P9-DNP-438

Leading in Turbulent Times

Leading in Turbulent Times

Kevin Kelly and Gary E. Hayes

BK®

Berrett–Koehler Publishers, Inc.
San Francisco
a BK Business book

Berrett-Koehler Publishers, Inc.
235 Montgomery Street, Suite 650
San Francisco, CA 94104-2916
Tel: (415) 288-0260 Fax: (415) 362-2512 www.bkconnection.com

Ordering Information

Quantity sales. Special discounts are available on quantity purchases by corporations, associations, and others. For details, contact the "Special Sales Department" at the Berrett-Koehler address above.

Individual sales. Berrett-Koehler publications are available through most bookstores. They can also be ordered directly from Berrett-Koehler: Tel: (800) 929-2929; Fax: (802) 864-7626; www.bkconnection.com

Orders for college textbook/course adoption use. Please contact Berrett-Koehler: Tel: (800) 929-2929; Fax: (802) 864-7626.

Orders by U.S. trade bookstores and wholesalers. Please contact Ingram Publisher Services, Tel: (800) 509-4887; Fax: (800) 838-1149; E-mail: customer.service@ingrampublisherservices.com; or visit www.ingrampublisherservices.com/Ordering for details about electronic ordering.

Printed in the United States of America
Berrett-Koehler books are printed on long-lasting acid-free paper. When it is available, we choose paper that has been manufactured by environmentally responsible processes. These may include using trees grown in sustainable forests, incorporating recycled paper, minimizing chlorine in bleaching, or recycling the energy produced at the paper mill.

Cataloging data is available from the Library of Congress.

ISBN 978-1-60509-540-0

First Edition
15 14 13 12 11 10 10 9 8 7 6 5 4 3 2 1

'It is not the critic who counts: not the man who points out how the strong man stumbles or where the doer of deeds could have done better. The credit belongs to the man who is actually in the arena, whose face is marred by dust and sweat and blood, who strives valiantly, who errs and comes up short again and again, because there is no effort without error or shortcoming, but who knows the great enthusiasms, the great devotions, who spends himself for a worthy cause; who, at the best, knows, in the end, the triumph of high achievement, and who, at the worst, if he fails, at least he fails while daring greatly, so that his place shall never be with those cold and timid souls who knew neither victory nor defeat.'

Theodore Roosevelt, speaking in Paris, 1910

In loving memory of Margaret A. Kelly

Contents

Chapter summaries

CHAPTER 1 All change

Thanks to the three Cs of credit, commodities and confidence, weather patterns have shifted from high growth to high risk. What are the driving forces behind the turbulent headwinds of change? What do you need to know and do about them? And how and when did change become a constant corporate reality?

CHAPTER 2 Knowing when the winds are coming

The first step in leading your way through turbulence is to recognise the early signals. If your radar is on, you can anticipate the degree and intensity of shifts in your marketplace and your organisation. But to pick up the signals you have to avoid Group Think; promote open debate; bring in outside perspectives; and carefully monitor your own reactions as you negotiate the turbulence ahead.

CHAPTER 3 All hands on deck

As turbulence approaches, you have to mobilise each and every person in your organisation to respond. This demands clear and realistic communication about the need for change; mobilising leaders to support the change; walking the talk to prove you are living the change; and maintaining your own energy levels.

CHAPTER 4 Navigating a new route

Building a new strategy is the next stage in negotiating the relentless headwinds. This requires a delicate balancing act. You must incorporate best practice ideas while building on what was already great about your organisation. You must manage risk while facilitating growth; create a sense of ownership for the strategy within the leadership team; and communicate the strategy and its implications for each part of the organisation.

CHAPTER 5 Mastering mutinies

Even when times are tough, some people are resistant to change – no matter how essential it may be. If you are to master potential and real mutinies you must first identify where the resistance is coming from. Then you must engage with the resistors – rather than attacking them. At the same time, you must nurture and encourage change leaders and provide motivation for the many rather than be derailed by the mutinous few.

CHAPTER 6 Learning to tack

Faced with turbulence, you must learn to change direction swiftly and decisively. You and your organisation must be designed to make swift decisions about modifications and changes in direction. This requires that you remain open to new ideas and observations; that communication flows constantly; and that you resist the creation of sacred cows.

CHAPTER 7 Living with turbulence

All of this is intensely personal. Leading your people and your organisation through turbulent times means you have to dig deep.

What are the personal and emotional implications? How can you cope and learn to thrive?

CHAPTER 8 The leading in turbulent times checklist

In distilled form, what do effective leaders in turbulent times to do so well and how?

Introduction

The business world is in the midst of a period of turbulence not seen for a generation. Some commentators liken it to the Great Depression of the 1930s. Hopefully, that may be overstating the crisis, but there is no doubt that the credit crunch sent shock waves through the financial world. Venerable Wall Street institutions such as Bear Stearns, Lehman Brothers and Merrill Lynch have bitten the dust. And, what started as a crunch has become a more wide-ranging crisis, a series of shock waves hitting the world economy. The volatility of commodity prices, especially oil, and fluctuations in currencies are all part of a broader weather system affecting business everywhere.

In part, this reflects fundamental changes in the economic world order – as America's economic hegemony is eroded. In part, too, it is the hangover from a decade-long credit binge in the United States and other parts of the developed world. But whatever the underlying causes, many business leaders have little or no experience of trying to stay on course in these sorts of once-in-a-career turbulent conditions.

What a growing number of leaders are grappling with is a challenge that is central to economic survival and social progress in the twentieth century: How do you pick up signals on your leadership radar that allow your people to navigate through the sorts of headwinds that are buffeting organisations all around the world? How do you inspire and reassure your people that they can come through these difficult times? Most of all, how can you as a leader turn these headwinds to the advantage of the organisation to ride them to success? In short: How do you lead in turbulent times?

The turbulent pattern

While turbulence has attracted headlines and dominated the agenda over the last years of this century's first decade it is nothing new. Indeed, in our work with corporate leaders over the last 20 years, we have been struck by a recurring pattern. Time and time again we are asked to help new leaders cope with the increasing volatility of their marketplaces.

It isn't simply that these leaders are uncomfortable with ambiguity or change – indeed many of them are promoted precisely because of their ability to manage complexity. Rather, it is the uncertainty caused by the accelerating rate of change that these new leaders find hard to adapt to. Many simply find they are overwhelmed by the sheer unpredictability of the economic weather patterns moving through their industries. Over time, we have come to see these powerful forces for change as the corporate equivalent of headwinds, something which must be faced and navigated by leaders and those they lead.

A headwind is defined as: 'A wind blowing directly against the course of a moving object, especially an aircraft or ship.' The reality is simple: the headwinds are here to stay. And the headwinds are unrelenting. The leadership challenge of the next few years is learning to fly with such all-embracing turbulence.

It's a bit like trying to fly through a hurricane. It doesn't matter whether you are in a light aircraft or a Boeing 787 Dreamliner, staying on course in a headwind is tough. What the best pilots realise is that you need to know how to read your leadership instruments and change course sometimes to make headway. Sometimes, too, you need to know when to put the plane down on the nearest piece of flat land and sit out the storm.

In 2009, our fascination with the issues facing frontline leaders in turbulent times across a wide range of sectors – from banking to retailing – led us to embark on a series of interviews with CEOs and business leaders worldwide. *Leading in Turbulent Times* is based on insights from those revealing and candid interviews.[1]

What did we discover? Three really strong messages emerged from our conversations:

> **Passion rules.** Leaders are frequently and usually unfairly pilloried for taking the money and running. True, the financial benefits of running large organisations have never been greater, but the leaders we encountered aren't turned on by money. It is important, of course, but they are driven by a real passion for their business, their organisation and the people they work with. Turbulent times simply highlight this passion under an even brighter light.

1 All quotations unless otherwise stated are taken from author interviews.

'For a business leader, the more the environment changes, the more passion he or she should possess', is how Wang Jianzhou of China Mobile put it. Money is one-dimensional; with passion you can turn everyone on.

Take Kris Gopalakrishnan, one of the founders of Infosys. 'I am passionate about the company. This is half my life. All we have achieved, that we have today, is because of Infosys. There is a lot of ownership and pride', he told us. 'We see Infosys as a mechanism for bringing about change. This means bringing about change in the industry through new models. We are seen as a leader. We are able to bring change to countries because of the position Infosys has in India. There are 103,000 employees meaning good jobs are being created. There are a lot of ways we can bring about change. People listen to you. You can influence government and society. We see Infosys as an instrument for change.'

Hard times call for mastery of the soft side. The so-called 'soft' skills of leadership – communication (which includes both informing people and listening to them and their concerns); empathy, which is not to be confused with sympathy but rather is a rigorous attempt to understand one's employee's views and efforts; and mentoring and coaching so that they feel that even in, or especially in turbulent times they are continuing to learn and develop – are vitally important in negotiating any protracted period of turbulence.

The hard stuff of keeping costs under control and slashing numbers tends to grab the headlines, but the leaders we spoke to were focused on guiding, helping and maximising the human potential of those in their teams rather than employing twenty-first century slash and burn tactics. This is a timely reminder that cost control is a business basic, but extracting great performance from people is always based on more complex and subtle motivational tools than pure fear.

Communication filled many pages of our notes and hours of our conversations with leaders. Communication is what leaders do. Day in, day out, they communicate. During difficult times all put a premium on the transparency and frequency of their communication internally and externally. Keeping the troops informed helps to decrease rumours and needless worries, while listening to their concerns and ideas keeps them engaged and committed.

'I create more opportunities than before to communicate with new guys directly – having lunch, breakfast, even dinner with them. I'm very close to them. They haven't had any experience of this kind of crisis or hard times before. So that's why I have to talk with them. I'm always there with them', says Takeshi Niinami of the Japanese company, Lawson.

Think long term. The moment can appear all-embracing as one wave of misfortune after another crashes down. Leaders refuse to bow under immediate pressure. Instead, they use short-term pressures to harden their focus on long-term objectives. While the present can appear confused and chaotic, for most inspiring leaders the future remains crystal clear.

'Clarity of vision, purpose and values make a CEO's job a lot easier because you never lose sight of what that long-term vision is and nor do your people – especially because you're always reminding them of what it is', says Linda Wolf, retired Leo Burnett Chairman and CEO. 'Having a long-term vision doesn't mean that you're complacent; in fact, it challenges you because you can always do better against it. At the same time, it gives you the clarity of purpose that is critical.'

Leading in Turbulent Times explains how some of the world's best leaders navigate through the eye of the storm. We hope this book will help arm all who read it with new perspectives on the challenges set to dominate corporate and leadership agendas for the years to come.

Kevin Kelly and Gary E. Hayes
July 2009

1 All change

'My own world has changed. I just don't think we will be able to put the genie back in the bottle. There will be a new business order coming out of all of this.'

Henry Fernandez, president and CEO of MSCI Barra

The universal truth of change

Fast, turbulent, mind blowing, exciting, scary. It has never been more difficult to make sense of the world.

Change rules. 'Our sales are half what they were this time last year, which is a challenge. But I think we're in the same place that a hell of a lot of other people are in right now', one CEO told us. 'The focus on performance is finer. When you are growing at 35 per cent everybody benefits; when your growth goes down to 11 per cent or 12 per cent, the separation between the poor and the best performers increases. And then you need to figure out how to handle it, because in this environment you cannot let that rise. We have had to let some of those poor performers go.'

Over the past three recessions in 1981, 1991, and 2001, the car rental company Hertz never experienced its annual sales contract more than 3.5 per cent in any given recession. In November and December 2008, it saw a 20 per cent fall. In January 2009, Hertz announced a reduction in its global workforce by 4000 employees in a bid to decrease costs due to reduced rental demand. Hertz had already reduced its workforce by 22 per cent in the past two years.

Change rules. It took the Indian company Infosys 23 years to reach revenues of $1bn and just another 23 months to hit $2bn. Amazing, but even more so when you consider the company's birthplace and the changes it, too, has witnessed. Ask any Indian leader and they will tell you that running a business in India before the economic reforms of the early 1990s was an impossible obstacle course – companies often had to wait a year to get a telephone line and individuals needed to give two weeks' notice of plans to fly overseas.

Change rules. 'When I got into this business in 1996 as a CEO, mainframes ruled, the Internet was just happening and nobody believed distributed processing would be as powerful as mainframe processing in years to come', says K. V. Kamath, CEO of ICICI Bank in India. 'Unless you keep yourself updated you will be obsolete. One good thing that comes out of me trying to reinvent myself is that it is easier to tell my colleagues that unless they also reinvent themselves they will be obsolete.'

Change rules. And rules change.

Another CEO told us a few years ago he used to get his

sales figures every month. Then it went to every week. Now it can be every hour.

In the next year, General Electric will launch more new products than in any previous year in its century-plus history.

'The environment has changed so much, especially in the financial sector, that some of the old rules do not apply', Bijan Khosrowshahi, former CEO of Fuji Fire and Marine in Japan observed, echoing the opinions of many in the business world and beyond. 'The old orthodoxies will not serve us well in the future', British Prime Minister Gordon Brown told the G20 Summit in spring 2009.

'For business leaders and people who are on the track to leadership, this will have a permanent impact on the way they do business. The level of trust has been diminished and I think it will take years and decades to build that back. In terms of how people are going to do business, I think there's going to be a lot more scepticism', anticipates former Leo Burnett CEO, Linda Wolf.

Change rules. Change is a fixture. There is no escaping this essential fact. Change rules. Charles Darwin said: 'It is not the strongest of the species that survives, nor the most intelligent that survives. It is the one that is the most adaptable to change.'

So, the first message of this book is that change is a universal fact of organisational life. No business is immune. Any leader who refuses to accept that change is inevitable in our turbulent times is in denial. Becoming an agile leader – in terms of thinking and behaviour – is critical for success in turbulent times. Rigid and inflexible thinking runs the risk of making today's leader irrelevant.

Going, going ...

How leaders manage, direct and communicate change has fascinated us for many years. We spoke to a CEO in Germany, and he observed that whenever a leader talks about change, employees always expect the worst. But, as a leader, how do you direct change for the good of the organisation and the people? How do you change things when your very survival as an organisation depends on it?

The best leaders we have encountered take change as their constant mantra. They live and breathe change because they know that the reverse of change is stagnation and then inevitable decay. If you sit still, pretty soon you are steamrollered.

There are no exceptions. Even a bellwether brand like Coca-Cola has had to wrestle with the highest percentage increases for oil, plastic, aluminium and sweetener of the last 50 years.

Take Christie's. It is the world's leading art auction business. Its New York building features a soaring triple-height entrance with a spectacular specially commissioned mural by the artist Sol LeWitt. The firm's global auction and private sales were more than $5.1 billion in 2008. One would have thought it is somehow insulated from the process of change. Art, after all, endures. Nothing could be further from the truth. The auction house is venerable, but its market has changed hugely over the last decade. It used to be that you could send a valuer round to somebody's estate to look at their pieces of art. The process was leisurely and local. Now it is truly global. Add in the effect of the Internet and the emergence of new wealth, and Christie's is in a fast-moving, turbulent marketplace.

Edward (Ed) Dolman, CEO of Christie's International, started out as a porter in the furniture department, rose to become an auctioneer and then decided he wanted to become a manager. He was appointed CEO in December 1999. 'The auction business is unique. We are dealing with high-value, totally subjective assessments, in markets that fluctuate widely. It is difficult to think of true parallels in other sectors', he told us. 'I don't think the governmental and political climate matches commercial reality. With the G20 and things like that, you can see attempts being made to come to terms with the fact that every economy in the world is now linked to such a degree that individual decisions taken by individual governments are fairly meaningless on their own and have to be coordinated globally. As a business, that reality is mirrored in our experience.' Change is constant and global.

Advertising change

Another business in the frontline of change is advertising. Often regarded as a barometer of the economy, advertising budgets are famously fickle. Today, too, the industry is undergoing a major paradigm change as it wrestles with the move to online advertising and issues of privacy. One of the most informed voices on the forces of change is Linda Wolf. She is now a director of Wal-Mart, and was formerly chairman and CEO of the ad agency Leo Burnett Worldwide. When she was promoted to become CEO of Leo Burnett in 2001, she became the first woman to run the iconic Chicago advertising agency – and one of the few to run an international agency anywhere. Wolf gained a reputation as a client-pleaser and a rainmaker. When she ran business development at Leo Burnett in the 1990s, she helped bring in clients such as Disney and Coca-Cola. She's known for going the extra mile to understand clients: in 2000, when she ran Burnett's US business, she went on a parachute jump with her new client, the US Army.

The metaphor of a parachute jump is worth adding to the metaphorical mix of these troubled times. But if it gets you a client, who can argue? (Though this comes with a leadership health warning: if you attempt a high stakes jump while trying to remain too rigid, you will break your leg or worse.)

At Leo Burnett and as a member of the board of trustees of Janus Mutual Funds and Wal-Mart, Linda Wolf has had a front row seat on the true nature of change. In conversation, she points out that the ongoing period of turbulence should be viewed as an accelerator of change rather than a sudden and discrete period of change.

In advertising and media, for example, turbulent change has been going on for the last decade as the market recalibrates online and printed content, and as traditional advertising and content companies vie with new media companies. (As we were writing, the *Boston*

Globe reported operating losses of $50 million for 2008, forcing the newspaper to contemplate what its future looked like.)

Says Linda Wolf: 'Everyone's trying to establish how you can make it through this process and still generate the kind of revenue you're used to. I was at a lunch recently and a big advertiser was saying, of course, we're using all this new media and that's where the opportunities are. Another said the bulk of what they did was on television; it still had the biggest impact for them and was where the bulk of their revenue went. I don't think anyone has cracked the code, and it's going to continue to evolve over a long period. It's a really tough dilemma for whatever media company you're talking about.'

If the times are challenging for the advertising industry, they are even more so for the traditional media companies. If you are a newspaper or terrestrial television company, for example, imagine how you feel about Google and YouTube. In the media world companies are trying to experiment with every possible new way of communication, and hoping that they're going to be able to own something in that area. Some of the experimentation is interesting and has huge potential – for example, Hulu (the free online video service) was a very smart thing for NBC to become involved in. As the experiments go on, traditional media – such as newspapers – continue to struggle with the forces of change.

One of those caught in this maelstrom of uncertainty is Tom Glocer, CEO of Thomson Reuters. 'When there's a disruptive change to your industry, you can't smooth your way quarter by quarter to get there. It takes a human and capital dynamo like Rupert Murdoch to take the *Wall Street Journal*. You can't smooth your way and that's the core issue in the media and places like the *New York Times* and the *Wall Street Journal* as they struggle to replace analogue dollars with digital pennies.'

Right now, business leaders in all industries are being buffeted on all sides by the forces of change. The headwinds of change we have seen, and will continue to see, can be loosely grouped under four categories: technological; organisational; macro-economic and political; and global.

Technological change: cognitive agility

One of the new breed of leaders we talked to was Alexey Mordashov, CEO of the Russian steel-giant Severstal. In the week that we talked with Mordashov he had started in Moscow and then visited Detroit, Pittsburgh, Frankfurt and Berlin, before returning home. A young, energetic leader such as Mordashov embodies the changes which we have seen over the last decade. Ten years ago the emergence of powerful and immensely rich Russian leaders wasn't on the agenda. Now, Russian entrepreneurs and multinationals rub shoulders with the most powerful Western business leaders and their organisations. Ten years ago some businesses were global; now it is difficult to imagine a large company that doesn't have global operations. And a decade is a long time in the life of technology. Alexey Mordashov travels the world, but is constantly in touch with his colleagues and offices via his ubiquitous pocket PC, laptop and mobile phone.

Technology has changed the job of leadership. It opens up previously unimagined channels of communication and new marketplaces. And technology has played a pivotal role in the creation of a galaxy of now global markets. Try thinking of a market untouched by technology or a leader whose work has not been touched by technology. We bet you're struggling to think of one!

For leaders to make good technological decisions they need to remain continuously informed about innovation and also to be well advised on the significance of technological advances for their business. Quick and serious cognitive processing is required.

Organisational change: interpersonal effectiveness

The second headwind that leaders have to cope with is organisational change. 'We need to be much more flat, creating a collegial team-based leadership style so that you can leverage a lot more of people's intellects and capabilities and make them participate in decision making', says Kris Gopalakrishnan the CEO and one of the seven founders of the global consulting and IT services company Infosys.

Both excellent social skills and keen emotional intelligence are required to build and exercise influence in a collegial high-performance organisational culture.

Organisations have changed hugely over the last decade. They have had to. Today's employees are less malleable. They refuse to be easily corralled by hierarchy or organisational boxes. They ask questions. They push the boundaries all the time.

Henry Fernandez, CEO of the financial services company, MSCI Barra, told us that though his organisation wasn't numerically large it was filled with highly-educated, smart and questioning people. About 10 per cent of his people have PhDs, another 30 to 40 per cent have masters degrees of one sort or another. 'They figure things out very quickly. They tend to be more open to change but, on the other hand, they're smart and can become cynical and harder to change. You only have a few windows in a tenure as a CEO so you've got to really use them', says Fernandez.

Try leading a smart workforce such as at MSCI Barra and many other organisations in this knowledge economy by traditional command-and-control methods and you'd pretty soon hit a dead-end. Equally, try organising them into neat hierarchies and boxes on a chart and you'll encounter problems. As a result, new organisational models are continually emerging. Some have been made easy thanks to technology. Others are simply fuelled by human curiosity.

The Management Innovation Lab at London Business School, the brainchild of Professors Gary Hamel and Julian Birkinshaw, has chronicled some of the most innovative organisational experiments. Consider the following examples.

Happy Computers is a $6 million IT training company in London founded by Henry Stewart. The charismatic and unique Stewart has a track record as a campaigner and entrepreneur. Inspired by Ricardo Semler's book *Maverick*, he set out to create a truly different organisation built on maximising people, having fun and making money (not necessarily always in that order). At Happy, managers are chosen according to how good they are at managing (which Stewart rates as 'our most radical idea') and they are openly appraised by their own employees; new recruits are never asked for qualifications, and are chosen according to how well they respond to feedback on their training style; mistakes are celebrated; client satisfaction, currently at an industry-leading 98.7 per cent, is the single most important performance indicator. While the industry has contracted by 30 per cent over the last six years, Happy's revenues have doubled. Happy days!

Or consider another organisational pioneer: Topcoder is a $20 million Boston-based software company founded by Jack Hughes in 2000. Software projects from clients are broken down into modules, and each module is opened up to Topcoder's community of 120,000 programmers as a competition. Open source meets open organisational design. Programmers are invited to complete the project within a set period of time. The developers of the best solution win a financial prize – typically in the tens of thousands of dollars – and the losers get nothing. For many top programmers the chance of winning a prize is far more motivating than being paid a steady salary. So by creating a tournament-based model for structuring work and rewarding effort, Topcoder is able to tap into their intrinsic desire for peer recognition.

Offbeat, you might think. But consider an experiment at Microsoft where Ross Smith, an 18-year company veteran has reinvigorated an 85-person test team in the company's Windows division. The testing team is young; its members live online, love competition, devour technology in any form and are avid readers of books like *Blink* and *The Wisdom of Crowds*. Ross Smith championed a number of initiatives to engage with his team – competitions, pizza meetings, book groups and more. His approach is driven by recognition and respect and has been described as when Theory Y (the notion developed by Douglas McGregor[1] that people perform best when their work is fulfilling) meets Generation Y.[2]

Travel the corporate world and you will encounter many other such examples of leaders pushing at the organisational boundaries, subtly and powerfully changing the shape of organisations.

Macro-economic and political change: quick and critical reasoning

The twentieth century was the American century and it is widely anticipated that this century will see the nexus of power shift.

The last 20 years have been tumultuous. Since the collapse of communism, the world has been redrawn and re-energised. Countries have come blinking into the economic light, one after another. More is likely to follow.

1 Douglas McGregor, an American social psychologist, proposed his famous X-Y theory in his 1960 book *The Human Side of Enterprise*, McGraw Hill Higher Education, 1960.
2 Julian Birkinshaw and Stuart Crainer, 'Game on', *Business Strategy Review*, Winter 2008.

'The rate of change in the world and the response time in volatility have increased dramatically. I think we need to adjust our thinking to how dramatically that has happened', says Victor Fung of the Li and Fung Group, the Chinese multinational founded in Guangzhou in 1906. 'A lot of people say, hey, this is a once in a century type of a problem. We haven't had anything like this since the 1930s. You hear all these statements, and they seem to imply that this is once in a lifetime, after I get through this one, boy, am I glad I will never have to face this again. But I'm not so sure. I think we are seeing both the compression of cycle time – how quickly the cycles come and go – and also the amplitude of the swings getting more and more severe. The world has fundamentally changed.'

A critical and agile mind that can balance between the seizing of rapidly forming opportunities and simultaneously manage risk is fundamental to success. As we have seen, many leaders in financial services and beyond have failed to get this balance correct.

Globalisation 2.0: cross-cultural fluency

Familiar names are also changing their global game. Peoria, Illinois-based Caterpillar is one of those great unsung global success stories. With sales and revenues of $44.958 billion (in 2007), it is the world's leading manufacturer of construction and mining equipment, diesel and natural gas engines and industrial gas turbines. There's nothing sexy about its industries but, like its leadership, it is quietly and compellingly cosmopolitan. Much the same can be said of Peoria, the oldest settlement in Illinois. Visit the town's website and you will notice that it is available in six languages. Perhaps there's an international gene in the water.

Caterpillar CEO Jim Owens joined the company in 1972 as a corporate economist. He worked in Geneva, Switzerland in the 1970s. From 1980 until 1987 he was back in Peoria in the Accounting and Product Source Planning Departments. Then, in 1987, he became managing director of Caterpillar's joint venture in Indonesia. He held that position until 1990, when he was elected a corporate vice president and ran a Caterpillar subsidiary in San Diego. In 1993 he came back to Peoria as vice president and chief financial officer. In 1995, Owens was named a group president and member of Caterpillar's Executive Office. Over the next eight years as a group president, Owens was at various times responsible for 13 of the company's 25 divisions. In December 2003, the Caterpillar Board named Owens vice chairman and appointed him chairman and chief executive officer in 2004.

'It was invaluable for me to have lived and worked in Europe for five years. I lived in Indonesia for three years. I've travelled extensively in all the key countries', he says. 'I understand how business happens there; I know a lot of people. Now, I'm probably in Asia two or three times a year and Europe two or three times a year. I'm in Latin America once or twice a year. I think it's imperative to have a global perspective. To have lived and worked outside of your home country is an invaluable learning experience that no amount of travel will offset. There are multiple things you learn about how to work with a different government, with different business customers and dealers. You learn how to deal in a different language; you learn to be sensitive to cultural differences, tastes, preferences and ways of doing things and ways of communicating.

'So, if you're running a large multinational company, I think having lived and worked around the world is one of the more important aspects of preparation. You know, amongst my senior executive group, the vast majority of our officers have lived and worked in a country that they're not from; not travelled, but lived and worked.'

'Have business, must travel', is the new global mantra.

Global nomads

Cross-cultural fluency, which combines cognitive understanding of societal differences with emotional respect and appreciation for their significance, is a key competency for successful global leaders.

This was the message time and time again among the leaders we spoke to over the last few years. They were quietly fervent globalists. They sought out the common ground between people – no matter what. 'One of the great challenges is to create a homogenous culture, based on the infusion of different cultures, and help people to interact with each other', says Alexey Mordashov of Severstal. 'I don't see many cultural differences between countries. Of course there are some, but there are also some common elements.'

Most of the managers we talked to had amassed international experience. Yorihiko Kojima, President and

CEO of Japan's Mitsubishi Corporation, one of the biggest and most prestigious of the country's *sogo shoshas*, has been with the company since leaving university and has worked in Saudi Arabia and the United States as well as Japan.

Take Rick Goings, chairman and CEO of Tupperware Brands. 'We are global nomads. We don't really define ourselves by our nationality in the company. What's really good about that (I find) is that what we care about in the culture we've developed in the company has transcended nationalism, and it's even transcended religion', says Rick.

When Rick Goings returned to the States after being group vice president for Avon in Asia Pacific, it was the first time in Avon's 100-year history that an executive was sent overseas and came back to a more senior role! Previously an overseas posting had been a highway to nowhere. 'The worm has turned so much that we will not have a person in a senior role unless they've had that kind of experience', says Rick. 'It isn't about taking a trip to Seoul or Hong Kong or Paris or Budapest. It's about living there – not just being sequestered in an expatriate community – and that forever sensitises us to listen and understand. It's almost like your whole approach to life changes.'

There are a lot of people like Alexey Mordashov, Jim Owens and Rick Goings out there who have been shaped by their global business experiences. They are passionate believers that globalisation is a good thing – for individuals and organisations.

Increasingly, research supports this view. Leaders say that globalisation is making business more complex but is having a positive impact on their organisations, according to a survey of 1410 leaders in 45 countries, published by PricewaterhouseCoopers. Internally, the factors that led to increased business complexity for leaders to a large or very large extent included expanding their operations into new territories (65 per cent), engaging in mergers or acquisitions (65 per cent) and launching new products or services (58 per cent). Externally, complexity was driven to a large extent by international, national or industry-specific regulations, laws, standards and reporting requirements as well as by competitors' actions. Global growth is often centred on the BRIC economies: Brazil, Russia, India and China.

Global expansion presents several challenges for leaders to confront, including overregulation (64 per cent) and trade barriers/protectionism (63 per cent) as well as political instability (57 per cent) and social issues (56 per cent). But leaders view globalisation in a positive light, with 58 per cent saying it will have a positive impact on their firms in the next year and 63 per cent seeing a positive impact in the next three years.

Fast globalisation

Some of those we spoke to anticipate that the financial meltdown will actually accelerate the pace of globalisation. Says Henry Fernandez of MSCI Barra: 'If your profitability is under threat, you're going to do everything within your power to preserve it. One of the things that could end up happening is an even more rapid globalisation of your workforce. We're increasing our headcount in emerging markets very rapidly compared to what the plan was and I see other companies – IBM and others – doing that.'

Henry Fernandez is a truly global citizen in a global market. He was born in Mexico City, grew up in Nicaragua and has lived in Geneva, Switzerland. From 1976 to 1979 Fernandez was a diplomat in the Nicaraguan Embassy in Washington, DC.

Reflecting on his global career, Fernandez says: 'Having grown up in other parts of the world, you have an appreciation of how broken economies have gotten broken, how problems have occurred, how revolutions have happened, how human rights have been violated, how people have been abused in the labour force and all of that. Having a global perspective and understanding of what goes on in other parts of the world gives you a lot more leverage, a lot more flexibility. You're not in a closed economy. You're not in a box, but know that if you can sell this product here, you can sell it in Japan, France, Brazil or wherever.'

Henry Fernandez interprets globalisation and the reality of practising business globally in an infectiously positive way. 'God created the world in a diverse way to enrich it, not to create conflict. The global perspective gives you that.'

With more than 3000 clients in over 60 countries, and 800 employees located around the world, MSCI is a leading global provider of investment decision support tools, including indices and portfolio risk and performance analytics. Henry Fernandez was instrumental in the design and execution of MSCI's acquisition of Barra in 2004, and in the merger of MSCI with Capital International Perspective in 1998. Prior to becoming CEO of MSCI in 1998, Fernandez was a managing director of Morgan Stanley, where he worked from 1983 to 1991 and from 1994 to 1998.

Henry Fernandez believes that one of the ultimate side effects of globalisation is the likelihood of an increasing number of economic bubbles. 'We're not going to reinvent the human race', he reflects. 'People go from fear to greed and in an environment where people were making a lot of money, then greed takes over and they get excited. So, the business cycle is here to stay as long as the human race is here. The psychological cycle of individuals is here to stay. What has accelerated the base is that globalisation has created an environment that is very prone to bubbles.'

Henry Fernandez is right. It is easy to underestimate the power of our interconnectedness. Equally, it is easy to forget that we are really in the early stages of the creation of a truly global business world. It is a work in progress. In the 1960s and 1970s there were three or four different worlds: the developed world – people sitting in the United States, Europe, Japan and a small number of other nations; then there was the developing world – countries like India, China and Brazil. They were completely closed and consequently lived in their own economic worlds. They were the economic equivalents of isolationist-communist Albania, managing to export things but little else. Then you had the impenetrable economic no-go areas of the Third World and the communist world. Now these worlds are unified and financial assets all over the world have been set free.

It is worth noting that markets for basic goods have actually remained fairly static. The market for copper is commensurate to what it was in the 1960s, but now money is truly global and the potential players in the market are also global. This means that a huge quantity of financial assets can flock into one fixed market and can take that market to extremely high levels of price, up or down. People can also borrow in one currency and lend in another currency and so on. With no global system of regulation – every country has its own individual system of regulation and people arbitrage that around the world – bubbles are, indeed, likely to become more frequent.

The answer is leadership

So what are the world's senior managers to do in the face of such unprecedented and unrelenting change? Confronted with change and its range of incredibly powerful drivers, there is one unifying need: leadership. When the going gets tough, the tough exercise leadership. Equally, tough times call for soft skills. Make no mistake – in turbulent times, leadership is the prerequisite of survival and future success.

'There's a huge difference between managing and leading. The world is full of managers. They're critically important in organising, processing, controlling, making sure that things are in place and on time', John Brock of Coca-Cola told us. 'Leadership's very different and finding people who are true leaders as opposed to managers is incredibly important. Leaders think about the future as opposed to the past; they think about how things *could be* as opposed to how they are. They think about people and the kinds of things that they could achieve or might achieve if they were given the right kinds of frameworks and principles within which to work. Then they take those people and really stretch them, put them into jobs that they're probably not quite ready for ahead of time, and stay just close enough to them to give counsel and guidance. That's my sense of how you really develop world class leaders. If I look at the times I have felt that I was successful, it's generally because I've had people around me who were outstanding leaders who were smart, often smarter than me, and who had developed outstanding leadership capabilities. That's what you've got to do if you're going to win.'

The courage of leaders

'What I always tell my managers inside Thomson Reuters is when things are going well it's easy. Customers are calling. You just answer the phone and take an order. Everything seems great. The results are great. You see positive numbers that make you feel good. Papers give you an easy time and nobody begrudges paying you your bonus or share awards because the performance is there, but, of course, all boats are being lifted by that tide', reflects Tom Glocer of Thomson Reuters. 'Conversely when things are rough outside, it tests who you are as a leader. You're cutting costs. You may be firing people and retiring them earlier than they want to. There's a lot of stress. The results don't look nice. The numbers sometimes have minus signs. And guess what? At a time when you're getting the least job satisfaction, you've got people saying, well, you shouldn't get a bonus because a bonus is for good results. So you're in this ironic position of working harder and having less to show for it and so potentially you've got a lot of dysfunctional emotion coming out. This is the time to test what you are really made of.'

Just as importantly, the difficulties of leadership should never be underestimated. Leadership is tough. In a modern organisation exercising leadership is a serious, time-consuming, tiring, demanding, exciting and rewarding experience. At the top there are no half measures. You don't climb half a mountain. You don't take in half a view. You don't address half an audience. You can't run any significant organisation, part of an organisation or a team of people, unless you are prepared to give enormous and whole-hearted commitment.

Stephen Langton is global managing partner of Heidrick & Struggles' Leadership Consulting practice. Steve argues that leading in turbulent times requires a brand of leadership courage. 'Most organisations have defined leadership capability lists that sound powerful but would be barely recognised as important in environments where real leadership is required. It is indicative that in the corporate world we have to define leadership values and principles. In environments which truly require leadership, its presence or absence is absolutely clear', he observes. 'The difference is courage. Moral courage. The courage to feel fearful but to present confidence and hope; to be honest and lead with truth. The courage to make decisions for your people not for yourself. The courage to challenge the principles, behaviours and values that created the status quo. The courage to be true to yourself and lead when it can be the loneliest position in the organisation.'[3]

We found courage evident among many of the leaders we encountered. 'I can't do the job half way', one executive told us. 'This is a do it all the way or step aside and let someone else do it job. A lot of people wouldn't be willing to do that. On the other hand, there's no shortage of people who want to take on the challenge. By the time you get to the executive office, there are a lot people who've dropped out along the way, who've said hey, I'm not willing to move around the world, I'm not willing to make the time commitments to this.'

Leading in turbulent times demands total dedication and belief. This was brought home to us when talking to Jim Skinner, CEO of McDonald's. When Jim became CEO he was the company's third leader in seven months after Jim Cantalupo and Charlie Bell. He brought with him the dedication and enthusiasm of a true believer. 'If you can't believe in your brand, you can't do your job with enthusiasm. I believe strongly you work for your company; you don't work for the boss. And I always felt that paid great dividends in McDonald's, not only in terms of my ability to contribute, but the support I received from the leadership of the organisation – or, as our former chairman used to say, if we all agree all the time, then we don't need one of us. I love the company, what it stands for, what we mean to the public, what we're responsible for, and what we're accountable for delivering.'

3 Stephen Langton, *Time for Leadership Courage*, Heidrick & Struggles, 2009.

It is reassuring when you meet up with someone like Jim Skinner. The commitment and belief is infectious. The lure of leading in turbulent times, as you will see, is not about money. It is about changing things. It is about beating the odds. It is about making a mark. It is about stewardship. It is about testing yourself in a leadership role during one of the most challenging times of the last century.

In times like this leadership matters. Leaders can – and should – make an incredible difference to an organisation. Professor Nitin Nohria and colleagues at Harvard Business School found that the leader accounts for 14 per cent of a company's performance (based on examination of a group of companies that had an average of three CEOs over 20 years; interestingly, figures ranged as high as 40 per cent for the hotels sector).

Other research found that nearly 50 per cent of a company's reputation is linked to CEO reputation (based on a survey of 1155 business leaders in the United States). Harvard's Rakesh Khurana estimates that anywhere from 30 to 40 per cent of the performance of a company is attributable to industry effects, 10 to 20 per cent to cyclical economic changes, and perhaps 10 per cent to the CEO. Ten per cent is still a great deal for one individual to be responsible for.

In turbulent times leadership can make the difference between survival and biting the corporate dust. Multiple and balanced skills with true passion make up the hard to duplicate leadership equation for success.

Resources

Rob Goffee and Gareth Jones, *Clever,* Harvard Press, 2009

Gary Hamel and Bill Breen, *The Future of Management*, Harvard Press, 2007

Henry Stewart, Cathy Busani and James Moran, *Relax! A Happy Business Story*, Happy, 2009

2 Knowing when the winds are coming

'I've been practising Japanese martial arts since university and one of the concepts you pick up is that you learn to read energy, people energy, body energy. You see the person, he's going to move, you see a punch, you see a kick, you see everything, but there's something else and by beginning to read that something else gives you a competitive advantage.'

Bijan Khosrowshahi, Fuji Fire and Marine

Cash up-front

K.V. Kamath is chairman of ICICI Bank, the biggest private sector financial services group in India, as well as being the country's largest private equity player, the biggest life insurance and general insurance company, and the third largest asset management firm.

As we spoke, K.V. Kamath was preparing to become chairman of the company, having been CEO since 1996. It was a mark of his leadership style and achievement that he was handing over to a 47-year-old woman who had risen up through the bank. K.V. Kamath's entire business philosophy is built around creating a meritocracy, encouraging young talent and promoting superior performers to powerful positions at an early age. His commercial insight can be neatly summed up as speed equals capital.

And he puts it to work. Back in July 2007 ICICI raised capital. Indeed, while other financial groups carried on with business as usual, it doubled its capital.

'What really struck us at that point was things were getting hot in the commodity price cycle, with a proliferation of products, signals from the West on property prices and the situation on the property front', K.V. explains. 'Nobody thought there would be a crack in the whole setup. We thought we would be better off preparing ourselves with healthy levels of capital. So we shocked the market. It was a bold decision and, of course, some of my colleagues resisted it, but we had the support of the board. In hindsight, it was the right decision because through this crisis, we have not really had the need to look at equity at all.'

Forearmed is forewarned

While ICICI was making bold decisions, which set it apart from the competition, few other companies made adequate provisions for the fallout when it emerged. 'The people who are moving through this with less angst and less damage are the ones that probably prepared better from the beginning. People didn't recognise the magnitude of risk that was out there', says Leo Burnett's Linda Wolf.

Only a select few saw it coming. Among them was PricewaterhouseCoopers, the global auditing firm. Former Global Chief Executive Officer of PwC Sam DiPiazza told us: 'Five years ago, we pulled back from sub-prime lenders because we were concerned. We're auditors, we looked at that and said, do we want to audit sub-prime lenders? And we said, there's too much risk, based on the way we saw the business going. We began reducing our high-risk areas two years ago, because you could see that there was a cycle coming, especially in the big developed countries.

'When I look at some of the changes we made, they were painful for our people. We didn't couch them in terms of a global recession coming, we simply said, we want to be very prudent in the way we spend money, in the way we grow our businesses, we're not going to always be growing in double digits, no cycle lasts forever. So we're just going to be a little bit more prudent. We've got 150,000 people round the world, and I'd say 145,000 of them had no clue that we were slowing the strategy down. We hired fewer people, we didn't slow down our promotions, and we continued to admit people to partnership, but we went to the leaders and said, okay guys, ratchet it down a little bit, because we think somewhere out there this is going to slow down. In the big, hot markets like Eastern Europe and China, it was really hard to do, so they kept their pace going because the demand was so high, but in most of the markets we were able to just slow it down gradually and we didn't disrupt or disturb the line people.'

The art of such subtle anticipatory shifts is barely understood. Professor Richard D'Aveni of the Tuck

Business School in New Hampshire coined the phrase *hypercompetition* to describe the fast-paced nature of business as he saw it then. That was 1994 – before the Internet was widely known – and it has got a whole lot faster since. In fact, in his recent book *Beating the Commodity Trap*, D'Aveni describes today's environment as 'Hypercompetition on steroids!' His book is all about how nimble leaders can take steps to outmanoeuvre their competitors in turbulent times.

As he explains: 'Most executives I talk to are comfortable with the notion of seizing opportunities. They understand that a proactive stance is often far better than a reactive one. The problem is that they can't necessarily see the window of opportunity in time to take advantage. Anticipating moves in their markets is what many able executives struggle with. Too many feel like deer caught in the headlights of oncoming traffic.

'The questions I hear a lot are: How can we see the earthquake coming? When do we need to make the change? How can we tell what our competitors are going to do before they do it? The answers lie with anticipation.'[1]

Anticipation is a critical factor and one which has been notably lacking in recent times. In December 2007, David Owen, chief European economist at Dresdner Kleinwort Investment Bank, put the odds of a recession in the UK during 2008 at 50 per cent. By early 2009, Ed Balls (former chief economic adviser to the UK Treasury) commented: 'The reality is that this is becoming the most

1 Richard D'Aveni, *Beating the Commodity Trap*, Harvard Press, 2010.

serious global recession for, I'm sure, over 100 years, as it will turn out.'[2]

The point is that you have to be looking for the dips in the road, or the change in the direction of the wind. Some organisations and leaders are and were clearly better prepared for unprecedented turbulence. Some countries even fared better than others. While Iceland hit the banking buffers, nearby Norway was racking up a budget surplus of 11 per cent, saw its economy grow by 3 per cent in 2008 and upped its stock buying programme as shares plummeted around the world. 'The strongest man is he who stands alone in the world', said Ibsen.[3] Elsewhere, Chile also boasted a fiscal surplus of 5.2 per cent of GDP in 2008. Few other nations can compete with these levels of foresight.

Horizon scanning

There are two levels to preparedness: organisational readiness and individual sensitivity to the changing context.

Michael Jarrett of London Business School has carried out extensive research into why some companies are more successful at change than others. Jarrett and his colleagues surveyed more than 5000 real managers and leaders in over 250 companies across different regions, from Australia to Zimbabwe. The sample included financial services organisations, pharmaceutical companies, manufacturers, and a host of others.

2 Ed Balls, from a speech to a Labour Party Conference, February 2009.
3 Henrik Ibsen, *An Enemy of the People*, 1882.

Using advanced statistical methods, they identified five critical internal capabilities that made the difference to organisations' fortunes. In his book *Changeability,* Jarrett uses the metaphor of sailing to describe organisational readiness for change. He notes: 'We identified the difference between those that succeeded and those that did not: their *readiness to change.* By this, I mean the managerial and organisational preconditions and internal capability to change. We find these in the organisation's routines, processes, and implicit learning.'[4]

Two factors identified by Jarrett are especially resonant during turbulent times.

'Scanning the horizon: Senior management teams that constantly scan their strategic environment tend to outperform their less eagle-eyed counterparts. They run constant radar sweeps of their surroundings, using a variety of data sources. Detecting new trends in the environment is often a stimulus for change, and it means that managers plan contingencies as the environment changes rather than waiting until the storm reaches their bows.

'Making sense of the signs: You can tell a lot about the approaching weather by reading the clouds, changes in the wind, and the subtleties of the waves. This is also true in the corporate world. Trends and data from the external environment need to be absorbed and used in decision-making. Senior management teams that are able to draw accurate and incisive conclusions based on organisational routines and good judgement are more

4 Michael Jarrett, *Changeability – Why Some Companies are Ready for Change and Others Aren't,* Financial Times Prentice Hall, Pearson Education, 2009.

likely to achieve change. They are able to make sense of what is going on and interpret the implications of their environment.'

At an organisational level, many of the companies we talked to had elaborate planning and strategy calendars. Infosys, for example, runs scenario planning, three-year business plans, one-year budgets and quarterly revisions before budget.

Sometimes these processes have proved woefully incorrect, but to some extent this is missing the point. By their willingness to engage with the future these organisations were already better placed than their competitors fixated in the moment. It is worth remembering that complacency and arrogance are the two greatest barriers to forward-looking vigilance. Failing to listen to feedback from the troops is another related and repeated threat.

Looking to the future and exploring difficult and different scenarios is actually a thoroughly healthy sign in organisations. It is an antidote to hubris. Says Ed Dolman of Christie's: 'The art market has sharp ups and downs, so at no point did we ever think we were in some sort of gravity-defying journey upwards.' Commercial gravity means companies and leaders can go down as well as up.

Healthy futures

Among the most far-sighted was the American healthcare group, Kaiser Permanente. It talks of a nuclear winter and a winter storm scenario. A winter storm is when the weather gets really bad and nuclear winter is when absolutely the worst thing that could happen turns into reality. Every year, Kaiser's senior executives go away and consider the possibilities. What if that happened? How would they respond, how should they anticipate, how should they interact now to keep it from happening?

This is then translated into a risk flow chart capturing the things which could put Kaiser at risk. These might include Medicare cutting back on the amount of money it pays the company; new legislation; competitors doing certain things; adverse media events; and so on. Solid self-esteem gives a leader the confidence to resist hubris and grandiosity. As a result, they can be receptive to warning signs and be the trusted bearers of potentially bad news.

In 2009, the executive team looked back at the 2003 version of the risk flow chart, which accurately predicted that in 2009 Medicare would significantly cut Kaiser's reimbursement because of major funding problems. The Kaiser team also predicted that the stock market would collapse because the housing bubble would burst, that fuel prices would be too high, and that the US auto industry would sink into the dust. In fact – and uniquely among the executives and organisations we talked to – Kaiser accurately anticipated the recession. It realised that in a recession it needed a different product mix and required a price sensitive response because people wouldn't have any money, and the low price is going to win. Out of that winter storm scenario, Kaiser began planning a product offering that, in fact, turned out to be 10 per cent of its business and may rise to be 25 per cent.

As Kaiser CEO George Halvorson puts it: 'We're constantly looking out, we're constantly living in the mode of 3- to 10-year plans and the 3-year part of the agendas are really robust, robust and living.' A truly visionary leader not only has the creativity to look forward for new opportunities, but also has the wisdom to be on guard for unforeseen perils and risks.

True north

'I believe that remaining true to what I think and believe should be the stance to take in all that I do to perform my duties. Putting this into practice perhaps helps me avoid stress. I also manage to squeeze in time to spend with my family, however busy I may be', Kazuyasu Kato of Kirin Holdings told us.

This was a common theme among the leaders we talked to. There was a sense among the leaders that they were firmly grounded. They knew their own true north, what they stood for, what mattered to them. This was important day to day in their decision making, but it also made them acutely sensitive to potential changes in the future.

'I think the people who can fare very well through this kind of situation are those with a foundation of a strong culture, values and vision to rely on. That will always be true', says Linda Wolf. 'Strong leaders thrive in this kind of situation. It is interesting to see the people who take something like this and learn from it; and also, there are people who surprise you in that they're up for the challenge. You really see the people who have that inner core of strength to deal with it. There's some people who you might, in normal circumstances, think are strong and then when it comes down to something like this, it's amazing how quickly they can fall apart.' Without a true north you quickly become disoriented by changes in the weather and can't anticipate where the next bout of turbulence is going to come from.

Customer radar

At an individual level, leaders can also do a lot to anticipate turbulence. Some of this is almost unconscious; other elements highly deliberate and conscious. The ability to sense different situations, to tune into shifting contexts is one of those skills leaders have to acquire. They tend to have their own individual tools and techniques for sensing the moment – and anticipating a change in the direction of the headwinds.

Some spend time with customers. 'I've always spent a lot of time out with customers because to me that's what makes companies exciting. I'm not a huge stay inside the office and do four week reviews of tonnes of spreadsheets', says Tom Glocer of Thomson Reuters. 'Companies for me come alive by seeing customers playing with our own products and getting out to see our employees around the world. So I've increased my time with customers.'

Asked about how he spent his time as the then CEO of Pitney Bowes, Michael Critelli estimated that around 5 per cent was spent on board and corporate governance matters; 25–30 per cent on meetings – individually with people who worked with him, staff meetings and around 150 one-to-one meetings every year with people from all levels of the organisation; 5–10 per cent meeting with industry officials, politicians and other regulators; and 10–15 per cent in some form of interaction with customers. In addition, he attributed around five days a year to talking to shareholders, analysts and rating agencies, and his remaining time was spent on a variety of outside activities which somehow relate to his job. Whatever the split, it is clear that communicating with people inside and outside the organisation lies at the heart of the job description.

As we will see, at the heart of situation sensing is communication – both incoming and outgoing. One of the most adept situation sensors we encountered was Bijan Khosrowshahi formerly CEO of Fuji Fire and Marine. 'It's like having your antennas up so you can also perceive what's happening so you can adjust your message or how you are communicating if something is not working.'

In the next chapter we look at making the leap from anticipating change to communicating what needs to happen now as you encounter the realities of turbulence.

Resources

Richard D'Aveni, *Beating the Commodity Trap*, Harvard Press, 2009

Michael Jarrett, *Changeability!*, FT Prentice Hall, 2009

Nirmalya Kumar et al, *India's Global Powerhouses*, Harvard Press, 2009

3 All hands on deck

> *'My experience being a CEO for ten years is that you're much better off being transparent and communicating frequently with your employees as to what you're doing and why you're doing it.'*
>
> Mark P. Frissora, Hertz, Chairman and CEO

The art of letter writing

Every week George Halvorson writes a letter to over 160,000 people. The chairman and CEO of Kaiser Permanente writes a note celebrating something someone in the organisation has done. 'Usually the letters are about us as people, the people at Kaiser Permanente; these are the kinds of things that we do; these are our values; these are our accomplishments. They're typically things that are illustrative of a collective effort', he explains.

Halvorson has been in the letter writing habit throughout his career. His weekly letter has become a fixture over the last two or three years. Previously it was a 10- or 12-page quarterly letter, something he has been writing for 20 or so years since he ran a plant in Minnesota.

Named CEO and chairman in March 2002, Halvorson has over 30 years of healthcare management experience. Kaiser Permanente, founded 1945, is the US's largest non-profit integrated health plan, serving more than 8.6 million members in nine states and the District of Columbia.

The letters work. When we talked Halvorson had just come back from a reception in Richmond where two different people came up to him, said they were Kaiser employees and that they both read the letter every week and looked forward to it. 'They really appreciate getting a sense of what we're up to and what we've just done. We have won a number of diversity awards in the last month so my letter last week celebrated our diversity and celebrated the fact that we have been winning awards in that area. People get a sense of what our values are, who we are.'

Adding up the responses, George Halvorson calculates that he receives around 10,000 to 15,000 responses to his letters a year. 'People will tell me things that I don't pick up any other way. People will say, we're having a problem with our supervisor because she's doing XYZ. I get a sense of flavour and tone from what's going on in the organisation, and people feel very free to communicate directly with me on a very wide range of topics. I just had a letter from one of our employees who had an idea for how we could use the Wii machine to do health education. He sent it as a response to my weekly letter and it was a very nice set of thoughts. And so I'm passing it onto our product and health people; and I will tell him I've passed it on, so people know it doesn't just come in and disappear. People have a sense of free communication.'

Halvorson ranges widely. He wrote about a programme to prevent premature births and brought in his own experiences after his grandson was born weighing just 2.5 pounds (1.1 kilos). He wrote about Kaiser's hospice programme and his dying uncle. He wrote about joint transplants, pointing out that a failed hip transplant is a significant event in a person's life rather than a statistic. Next day, Halvorson received two letters. One was from a surgeon who said the letter had reminded him that his work touched people's lives. The other came from someone who had had their hip replaced and then had to have a new one put in. Halvorson sent the second letter to the surgeon to further reinforce the point.

There are broader points at work in George Halvorson's letter writing. First, it is a very personal form of communication. 'What I try to do in the letters is just communicate a sense that we're about people and we're about taking care of folks and that we're inherently a culture of caregivers', he says.

Halvorson regards communication as being at the heart of changing Kaiser's culture to one which is transparent. 'You start with one culture. Then you say: Where do we need to go? and then to get to that culture what are the intermediate steps? Because you usually can't just go from culture A to culture B if they're radically different; you have to go through intermediate steps to get people to understand the value and to buy into the value of the ultimate culture.'

As part of this process, Kaiser put together a cultural development chart. This was basically a five-year agenda to get to the end culture it wanted. It identified which things needed to change in year one, which things in year two, what sequence things had to work in, and how the various cultural attributes interacted. This was then synchronised with the operational plans for the company.

The culture of transparency is credited by Halvorson as a major factor in Kaiser being able to put in a $4 billion computer system – the biggest computer system implementation of any private company in the world. Instead of this massive new system change being imposed from the outside, before Kaiser started the programme Halvorson took 90 physicians and spent time going through the possible outcomes, forging a sense of shared vision, and then selecting which vendors could deliver which parts of that vision.

'By the time we started this $4 billion project, we had a whole bunch of really key, well placed people within the organisation who had a sense of what it was about, where it was going, why it was happening, and what the tool kits were', Halvorson says. 'And then we sat down, brought them all together again, we picked the vendors, picked the team, and we sat down together and did a collaborative build and then spent a couple more months with another set of people – some of the same people but some additional people – to do a collaborative build for how are we going to put these tools in place, what's it going to look like, how's it going to affect the hospitals, laboratories, whatever? And so we had this collective agenda, and then we went forward and set up the track and laid it out and delivered.'

As a parallel, the UK's National Health Service is attempting to introduce a mammoth medical record programme. This started at the same time as Kaiser's programme, has so far cost twice as much, and still doesn't work.

Elevator pitch

If leadership is the job, making change happen demands communication. Communication is an ongoing and huge challenge in any organisation and particularly when change is happening. 'During restructuring I took it upon myself to do daily recordings so people could call in and I'd do phone calls to the entire company on a regular basis. We'd send out updates on everything that was going on and it was never enough. You just cannot over-communicate', says Peter Sharpe, CEO of Cadillac Fairview.

One of the most open, frank and plain invigorating of the people we encountered was Tim Flynn, chairman of KPMG. His openness was disarming. First, he talked about whether he was the right man for the job. 'I'm not the only person in my firm that can do this job. I'm the only person that can do it the way that I do it, because everyone is unique in how they carry out these responsibilities. But there are other people who can do it. I think there are people who are right for certain times in an organisation and the key is how do you manage the right person with the right skill set at the right time in organisations. How do you match with the need of the organisation at that point in time?'

Tim argues that the higher you progress up the leadership hierarchy, the broader your span of accountability. Simply, there are many more things for you to get involved in. The question this poses is how good are you at delegating and what do you arrange your time to become involved with?

One thing Tim doesn't delegate is something he patently enjoys: reaching out directly to people in the organisation. 'The time I enjoy the most is out in front of our people', he says. 'I get the chance to talk to 1000 new hires at our orientation. I talk to my partners at the annual partners' meeting, meet with people one-on-one. I'll go to an office and walk around the halls and stick my head in people's office and say, hi, ask them what they're doing. And it's amazing, I'll get all these emails afterwards that'll say, gees, no-one ever did that before. The impact you have on people and the ability to bring faith to an organisation is powerful.'

At KPMG's New York HQ on Park Avenue the firm has a number of floors. This means there's a high probability that anyone in the elevator is from KPMG. If he's in the elevator, Tim Flynn keeps his eyes open. If someone pushes the number for one of KPMG's floors, he will ask if they're with KPMG and then introduce himself. 'They look at me and say, hi, and think, who's he … oh, my God! I'll say, what do you do, what's your role, and all this kind of stuff and, and have great conversations. That sort of thing buzzes around the organisation and you can see the impact.' Indeed, think of the impact: a chairman who is passionate about engaging with people and who takes every opportunity to do so.

This abiding passion for communication was probably the most powerful recurring theme among those we interviewed. Take Jim Skinner, vice chairman and CEO of McDonald's since 2004. He served nearly 10 years in the US Navy before beginning his career with McDonald's in 1971 as a restaurant manager trainee in Carpentersville, Illinois. Through his career he has held numerous top jobs. For Jim Skinner it doesn't matter whether you're running a restaurant or a corporation, it boils down to communication. 'I think the important thing, in the best of times and in the worst of times, is communicating a clear vision for the organisation', he told us. 'This leads to strategic intent, tactics and all those other kinds of things, but most importantly it is about who we are and what we stand for. We're in the food business, we're a restaurant company. We're focused on the customer. It all revolves around doing a better job today at what we have always done. We don't do anything else that can impact the interface with our customer, that makes money, anywhere in the world, except at the front counter and drive-through. Fifty-five million times a day this is critical. It is about staying the course. We're a brand that deserves to be trusted. And the good news is the communication doesn't change whether we're good times, or we're under heavy scrutiny, or there are issues.'

Jim Skinner's communication mantra is that less is more. 'I do use a BlackBerry, but that's because I don't want to carry a laptop. I use it just to stay in communication relative to emails and information, and sales, not necessarily to communicate, on important issues with people. But you have to be accessible, and I am accessible. People can reach out for me.'

Habit forming

Communication for Sam DiPiazza of PwC had to cover the 150 countries the firm operates in, 8000 partners, and a total of 150,000 people speaking 80 different languages.

'An old mentor of mine used to say that good habits in good times means good habits in bad times. The good habits that we've built are that we've got clear lines of communication and we've got structures and processes in place that can motivate the line of management that needs to be informed and can then touch the rest of the organisation. It doesn't feel the same in Russia as it does in Kansas. Kansas doesn't feel good, but Russia feels worse. Dubai feels nasty and so you've got to make sure that you're adaptable to different parts of the world that have different cycles or a different intensity.'

Communication PwC-style is a true trickle-down model. A group of very senior managers around the world – perhaps 200 in total – are incessantly communicating to the 8000 partners, and the 8000 partners feel a high level of ownership to about 10 or 20 people each. 'It's consistent, it's process driven through structures that are in place, and you ratchet it up to a higher level when things get difficult', summarises DiPiazza.

To give a sense of the levels of communication DiPiazza is in the habit of, when we spoke he had just come off a five-hour video conference which had begun at 7am. It featured participants from six countries throughout the world. 'People have to see that you're human, they have to see that you understand that's something changed, and that you acknowledge it, and then that you're listening to their input on how to deal with it. What we try to do in this time is to say to our people, we understand how you feel, because we feel the same way and this is what we're trying to do about it. Then you get feedback from your people through town hall meetings or telephone calls or webcasts and your people will give you their reactions. Some of it's pretty aggressive or nasty, but more often than not, if you include them, you can work your way through this.'

Communicating in turbulent times

Communication in turbulent times must follow a number of straightforward rules.

It begins with listening

Alexey Mordashov took his top team at Severstal away from the workplace to think about communication issues. It proved powerful and illuminating. The lessons, he told us, were clear: 'If goals are very simple and clear, we are able to communicate to each other, and to interact and to support each other and demonstrate enough trust to achieve goals very, very effectively. This showed us that what was missing for effective team performance was a shared vision about our goals. And also what appeared very clearly was that a lack of listening, was a major cause of tension. We just didn't listen to each other. It was very important guidance for us, to understand that we could act as a team, and a major area for improvement for us was just listening to each other. Listening has helped us better understand ourselves and what to do.'

At Heidrick & Struggles we produced a book of parables called *Listen*. There is one page which many consultants have framed on their office walls. It reads: 'As a partner and consultant you should follow your biological set up. Two ears and one mouth means listen twice as much as you talk.' That's a pretty good maxim for any leader.

The reality is that the more anxious people are, the less good they are at listening. The leader has, therefore, to find all sorts of ways to try to hold their interest and hold their attention.

It can be difficult, partly because people tend to keep quiet around their leaders. Listening tunes you into the audience, but there are often residual barriers. A Western executive working in Japan told us a story of how he went to a distant part of the country to sign an agreement with a banking group. He could speak Japanese but encountered a confused response. The Japanese banker had never dealt with a foreigner in his working life and was very nervous. Because the banker believed the foreigner was going to be different and difficult to communicate with, this was what happened despite the Western executive's endeavours to put him at his ease.

Similarly, when Bijan Khosrowshahi was CEO at Fuji he put listening centre stage – really listening. Historically, at Fuji meetings an executive would typically present a report by simply reading it out loud. The junior person would read the report word by word. Half an hour of the meeting was given over to reading a 3-page report. There would be a ten minute discussion and that was the end of the meeting. Khosrowshahi decreed that there was to be no more reading at meetings. 'Everyone does their reading before and we're just going to talk', he says. 'This was a huge, huge culture shift. People would come to the meeting with papers in their hand and I would literally tell them to put their papers down. I don't want you to read your papers. Tell me what the issue is. Tell me what's going on.'

Straight talk from the start

'The message is very clear, and you take the message down the organisation to every single employee', summarises K.V. Kamath of India's ICICI Bank. Sam DiPiazza of PwC struck a common theme when he was talking about communication. His message was that actually telling people the truth, being upfront and giving it to people straight, was the only way forward. Says DiPiazza: 'We basically said to our people, you see the reality, we see the reality, we're going to do our best to stay the course with you, but you're going to have to step up your game. Over the next 12 to 24 months, salary adjustments are going to be lower, bonuses are going to be lower, promotions are going to be slower, or the alternative is that we fire 6000 people.'

Hard messages. The obvious next question for us to pose was what happened? How did PwC's 150,000 plus people take it? DiPiazza explains. 'Our people basically said, OK, we'll work with you. When it becomes obvious to all your people that the business has shifted, you have to be open with them. You know, the business has shifted, we are moving from 8 or 9 per cent growth to 2 or 3 per cent growth. Most of our businesses are either growing 2 per cent or shrinking 2 per cent around the world. We told our people that while that's better than almost any other sector in the world – it is different. They are going to have to work in an environment that's a bit more stressful. In some of our units around the world, we told them, next summer, when we have salary adjustments, it's probably going to be flat, no salary increases, unless you're promoted. So our people know it's coming, and that takes all the edge out of it, you know, when there's no surprise.'

Tough times call for straight talking. If you take over a company in a muddle – or worse – there is little to be said for politeness and understatement. Talk straight and act in accordance with what you say.

'We have certainly started communicating internally in a very different way', says Ed Dolman of Christie's, 'with regular communications directed from me to the whole organisation about what's going on and how we're going to react to it. There is much more direct communication than we did before. We've done a lot of staff meetings, communication meetings, town hall type meetings, because rumour and fear are running rampant.'

The truth is that if leaders are upfront and honest then people tend to respond in kind. If things are tough, people tend to know that. 'Strangely enough, if people understand that you're in trouble, and that you're having to make tough decisions and this is what's driving these tough decisions, and this is likely to be happening in the next month or so, once people have heard it and got comfortable with the rationale and the way the decisions are being made and that sort of thing, hopefully it makes things more understandable to them, and there's less fear and there are less rumours as a result', says Ed Dolman. 'I think communication is absolutely key. But it is difficult to communicate in the world we're in now, where any form of digital messaging, whether it's rumour or video or anything, can go straight out to the public domain.'

At the British retailer Marks & Spencer, CEO Stuart Rose set about restructuring the company, concentrating on making cost savings of some £260 million. Six hundred and fifty of the 3500 corporate employees left. He felt it was important that his deeds matched his words from the very start. 'What I felt was that you had to talk the talk and say it as it was. And remember, we were fighting a bid at the time – so we needed to say it as it is, not only to the press whom we were trying to win over and get our point across to, but also internally. Because if you were saying it to the press you couldn't then not do something internally, so that again was an advantage because it gave me a double strength.'

It must be simple

'You need to ensure that everyone understands what it is they're working towards and what part they have to play in it. As a CEO, you need to be able to articulate a simple idea of where you're taking everyone and why. If you can do this, you will have a high chance of creating the kind of engagement that produces a cohesive team that delivers to the organisation's objectives', says Talal Al Zain of Bahrain Mumtalakat Holding Company.

'Whatever the message is, it is important to make it simple. Complex messages are never understood. The only things that are going to be effective are things that are simple. Then people around you can understand and act on them', says Carlos Ghosn. 'At Renault and

Nissan, we have three- to four-year business plans with a maximum of three commitments that the company sets to achieve in order to keep the focus and to enable limited and concrete milestones and objectives.'

Complicated messages are harder to decipher. If you can say something simply, then do. This includes eradicating management speak and jargon. The legendary US investment guru Warren Buffett once opined that if he doesn't understand something, he assumes that someone is trying to fool him.

Plain speaking is not easy. Many organisations are steeped in a culture of management speak. Failure to communicate simply can be costly, however. In 1983, computer manufacturer Coleco wiped $35 million off its balance sheet in one quarter. The reason: customers found the manuals for a new product line unreadable and swamped the company with product returns. In 1984 the firm went bust.

It must travel the world

Communication is now global and with this comes further capacity for confusion.

You can never assume that your audience is on the same wavelength. One of us went to a friend's 40th birthday dinner in the United States. His daughter was asked to set the table. It was explained that the forks needed to be on the left and the knives on the right with their sharp sides pointed towards the plate. She got the forks right, but the knives were carefully placed at right angles to the plate. The girl had been helpful and had listened, but the final detail of communicating wasn't thought through. Imagine the room for misunderstanding in a global organisation where there are, metaphorically at least, knives and forks everywhere.

Global communication demands ever greater precision. Confusion is often the product of ambiguity. Don't say: 'I want the project tomorrow.' Specify what project, where you want it, and at what time. Then there is much less margin for error. This way if you actually wanted the project on your desk in the morning, you won't spend the day stressed out because the person delivering it thinks they have until midnight to email it to you.

Bijan Khosrowshahi, formerly CEO of Fuji Fire and Marine, brings a unique perspective as one of the very few foreign CEOs who has led a Japanese company. Indeed, at Fuji he was the only foreigner among 6000 employees. 'English is my third language so I was often communicating in a language that is not my mother tongue to someone for whom English is also not their mother tongue and maybe I'm doing it through a translator whose mother tongue is also not English. You simplify your message', he says. 'When I gave a speech, whether it was a five minute talk, a big meeting, or 10 people, the translators want to have the outline and they want me to read it. That's one of the things I changed. I said no, I'm going to give you topics that I'm going to talk about, so they can be prepared but I'm going to look at people, I'm going to get a feeling what they think or where their mind is, and I'm going to adjust what I say based on that. It took some time but they understood that that is how I communicate and that was very effective.'

It needs to be personal

'I do a lot of little things that in my mind I think of as kind of cheesy. But they aren't cheesy and people actually appreciate it', Nick Stephan of Phoenix Partners told us as we discussed his communications style. 'Every day I probably spend at least an hour of my day wandering around the broking floor chit-chatting with some of the guys, how're they doing, how's their month going, how are things. I could pull up the dashboard and see how it's going, but I go out and give them the personal touch.'

Says Mark Frisorra of Hertz: 'I believe in times that are really tough actually touching and feeling and being with people, that personal touch, that experience of bonding and sharing information, and doing collaboration, provides energy when you need it the most.'

In the information age we have a huge choice of communication media – email, telephone, video conferencing, etc. But, evidence suggests that none are as effective as face-to-face interaction. About 80 per cent of human communication is non-verbal. Facial expressions, body language, eye contact – these are key conduits.

We read body language to pick up the atmosphere. We walk into a meeting and pick up the feel of what other people are thinking. We watch how Y reacts to what X is saying. You can't do that by video conference. Body language speaks volumes. Ignore it at your peril.

'I believe a word from my mouth, or from anyone, has a strong soul. If you talk directly instead of through email and as long as you have a strong will, you can convey your will. This is right, let's get things done,' says Takeshi

Niinami, CEO of Lawson in Japan. In the early days in his job, Takeshi estimates that he spent almost 70 per cent of his time talking and listening to people face to face.

Takeshi especially made use of team meetings. 'You can have direct communication with 30 or 40 people, rather than using email. Actually I didn't use email at all – I just spoke on my own with the people. And I was always there at our training programmes at the Lawson University to talk to managers directly. Even now, for probably three months of the year, I'm not in the office at all. I'm out of town and don't come back to Tokyo.'

Change and leadership begin with conversation. Bold decision making has to be backed by consistent and committed personal communication. Always. To sustain that time commitment to providing straight, clear information and to listen as openly as possible to your audience's concerns and reactions is harder than it may sound. It requires a leader to be able to draw on a deep well of self-esteem in order to remain balanced and be neither evasive nor defensive.

Flatter management structures mean that executives can no longer rely on hierarchical power to get things done. Instead, managers must increasingly rely on persuasion – and inspiration. This requires a more sophisticated style of communication directed at the individual and imbued with emotional context as well as content.

One survey of 60 executives found that the messages that get attention are those where the message is personalised, evokes an emotional response, comes from a trustworthy or respected sender, and is concise.

Great leaders have long been aware of this. Jack Welch of GE habitually sent handwritten notes to workers at all levels, from part-time staff to senior executives. Some even framed his notes, as a tangible proof of their leader's appreciation.

Seung-Yu Kim of Hana Financial Group told us about the amazing efforts he puts into establishing personal rapport with all the bank's employees. After Hana merged with several banks, Seung-Yu set out to memorise the names of as many people as possible. He memorised almost 1000.

'I had their photographs and their names, a CD in my car, and something on my desk, and even beside my bed. I tried to remember their names and their background, which province they came from, which school they graduated from. I tried to memorise them all. I also pop into branch offices whenever I can.'

It needs to be authentic

Your communication style not only needs to be personal, it needs to be authentic too. It needs to be your voice.

There's a great Dilbert cartoon. In it, the boss approaches the long-suffering technical writer and announces that he has decided to write a daily blog. 'Every day I will record my personal thoughts about our business', he declares, before adding: 'I need you to write the first one by noon. I can't wait to see what I'm thinking!'

We can all share the writer's dismay. Communication – whether it is by blog or more traditional means – is not something a leader can delegate. Of course, leaders need help with communication, but the sentiments communicated – be it good news or bad – should always be their own.

Regularity breeds contentment

'I've increased the pace and the depth of communication, making sure our staff know clearly what's the strategy and why we're not managing week to week and yo-yoing projects. That's probably the biggest change in my time', says Tom Glocer of Thomson Reuters.

The reality is that better communications could – and perhaps should – sort out most of the day-to-day problems in organisations. Poor communication is the consistent downfall of organisations – now and tomorrow. Effective leaders constantly communicate. Indeed, they often communicate exactly the same message but to different audiences. An appetite for repetition is part of any top job description. And the repetition needs to be consistent, for there is danger in varying the message, even slightly, for different audiences. If we send a message to our employees in one region, the global grapevine immediately kicks in and soon it is all over the company: the message must be the same for all.

'I've learnt that people don't get the message until you hear it back from them. Once they're starting to repeat the message, then you know, okay, they're on the team', says Sesame Workshop's Gary Knell.

Bruno Lafont, chairman and CEO of Lafarge told us he reads only direct emails but maintains constant communication in other ways. 'I meet with my executive committee team for three hours every week, and meet with each of them individually once a month for one hour, and when needed. Together, every month, we review the advancement on the Group's few strategic and operational priorities. We now have quarterly business reviews and I attend many of them. I keep travelling a lot and try to meet informally as many local employees as possible, which ensures that I have a good understanding of what is going on in the business.'

Leaders who are good communicators know it is essential to maintain a frequent dialogue with their executive team. It is no use hauling an executive in to give them a roasting if you haven't spoken to them for the previous month. Regular dialogue should have removed the need for the dressing down. And remember that communication is a two-way activity. Key to this interaction is listening. Always.

'The best advice I was given is you've got to work hard at being a good listener. The higher you go, the more important that is', says Caterpillar's Jim Owens. 'Most people who are highly successful are a bit of a bull in a china shop at some parts of their career. I had senior managers sit down with me, reviewing my performance and saying, here's an area that you ought to really work on. I did try to take that to heart and now I work very hard at creating a culture where people can feel very comfortable disagreeing with me. I want to engage in the fray and the debate. I want to get all their best ideas on the table, particularly my direct report team.'

One of the most striking examples of communication we have come across comes from Seung-Yu Kim of

Korea's Hana Financial Group. His willingness to open up communication channels with employees is deeply impressive. 'My people can send me emails at any time, even very early in the morning, two or three o'clock. They really appreciate it and that's why they try to listen to me.' At the company's training centre, training finishes at 9 or 10 o'clock in the evening. Seung-Yu Kim makes a point of taking the opportunity to talk to the groups of 30 or 40 people. 'I talk with them personally and meet face to face with the people. And then I accompany them to one of the nearby small bars and drink Korean liquor, *soju*. Actually I don't drink at all, so sometimes I drink water because the colour is the same! It is about hugging them one by one.'

When any of Hana's people are hospitalised, Seung-Yu Kim always visits them in hospital. As the bank has 12,000 employees this is no mean feat. He also always attends the funerals of the parents of employees. 'Our people are like my family', he explains. 'If they have some trouble, they call me up first.'

Be positive when you can

'Unfortunately, in a crisis most people focus on the negative. There is a group of people in any company – sometimes it may even be the majority – who just want to hear negative news. They want to lick their wounds. I refuse to do that', says Henry Fernandez of MSCI Barra. 'As soon as the downturn was apparent, I went out on the offensive telling people that a crisis is a terrible thing to waste. I kept telling everyone, look, this crisis presents huge opportunities, we want to take advantage of those opportunities. We went around the various departments

– we have about 800 people in 15 countries. We would email and call people and say, okay, what are you going to do for the business today that is going to be positive? Are we going to take market share away from competitors? Are we going to serve clients better? Are we going to come up with more innovative products to help people do risk management? We're going to keep the same level of investment, the company, but can we do more?

'If you look at the very macro picture of the global economy, the global equity markets, the global this, you will say there is no money to be made anywhere because everything is bad. But a lot of our business, like every other business, is made one client at a time, one purchase at a time, one investor at a time and therefore I will say, yes, there are a lot of people out there who are suffering and they don't have budgets and their assets have come down, but there are also a lot of people out there that have budgets to spend, so we're going to focus on that.'

It is tempting to slide into negativity. There is a lot wrong in any organisation – and that includes your own. No one you encounter is perfect – and nor are you. So, accentuate the positive and use positive reinforcement to back your strategies. This was brought home to us talking to Lawson's Takeshi Niinami.

One of his strategies was to make the company's local branches receptive to local needs rather than standardised by central dictates. 'We are everywhere in Japan and Japan has a very diverse culture and lifestyle. So we have to understand local customs and to match up with local customs. We can't decentralise customer needs', he says.

When the first stores started matching local needs, there was an expectation that the CEO would issue a reprimand. Standardisation had been the policy. Instead, Takeshi Niinami praised the efforts of the stores in front of as many people as he could. 'These kinds of things easily fly all over Japan', he says. 'Some products, local products or local rated products, were failures. But I didn't give them bad feedback. Basically, before I arrived people didn't want to challenge the status quo, they just listened to management. They never thought on their own. I just pushed people to think on their own.'

Negativity is corrosive. To stand any chance in the job, a leader has to quickly identify positive messages and continually emphasise them. Repetition of key positive messages is the hard graft of leadership.

Says Stuart Rose: 'We tried, often via some very simple things, to give people their confidence back because the morale of the business was very damaged. There was a feeling of inevitability about the fact that we were a mid-market retailer either going to be undermined by cheaper competitors, like Matalan and Primark, or be completely swamped by competitors with mass appeal like Tesco. We reminded people that this was not a new problem. We had had competition through the preceding 110 years of our history in different forms and different shapes and different places. This was just another manifestation of the same problem, but this time we just weren't dealing with it. So we used to go back and remind them what were the best things about Marks & Spencer. I still use that a lot. Quality, value, service, innovation and trust are the five words we always use, and the three most important things we need to do are to have better products, to have better shops and to have better service. I still use those five words almost every day in this business and I'm pretty certain now most people can remember them and say, actually he's got a point.'

Communicate up

Communication needs also to be channelled up the organisation. Even for CEOs this is an issue. The channel of communication between the CEO and the boardroom needs to be constantly open. In too many cases CEOs seek to communicate with their boards when problems are mounting. On the other side, boards are often tempted to spring issues on unsuspecting CEOs at board meetings. Gamesmanship helps neither side win the game.

The best CEOs spend time between the board meetings in touch with the board members, managing expectations, seeking advice, taking soundings.

Clear and regular communications can turn around problems. One Fortune 100 company's fortunes had declined over ten years. By the time its board looked for help it was in effect a turnaround. A new board with broader advisory skills took over, but within three years it became apparent that the new CEO, while effective at improving operations was not able to reposition the company's strategy. Eventually, another CEO was brought in. He created a weekly communication plan with the board to keep them abreast of the major strategic shifts and allowed an open forum in board meetings so that board members could witness first hand the executive team in action. In this case, open and consistent communication helped the nimbleness of the company's decision making.

Use technology, don't let it use you

We were talking to an executive and he told us about getting into bed one night with his BlackBerry – his wife turned to him, looked his BlackBerry and said, 'Only one of us is staying in this bed tonight.' Who says romance is dead?

Communication and technology are now intertwined. This cannot be ignored. Most of the effective leaders we encounter use technology sensibly and comfortably. 'At Hertz I issue a monthly email newsletter to all employees and host a quarterly global webcast. We're talking about what we're doing and why we're doing it. I also have a special email address so employees can communicate directly with me so I can answer their questions and act on their suggestions in real time' says Hertz CEO Mark Frissora. 'We cut the employee base from 40,000 people down to 24,000 people in a period of two years here. And I can tell you our morale on a lot of our locations is better than it was, so we feel good about that. But it's all due to just telling people what you're doing and why you're doing it, it's that simple. But you have to commit to that transparency, and to spending the time with people so they understand what you're doing. If you do that, it can be managed and managed effectively, without hurting the morale of the overall company.'

Jim Owens of Caterpillar echoes the thoughts of many we talked to. They were technologically savvy but wary of having their agenda hijacked by being available every single second of every minute of the day. 'I don't allow myself to be the slave of email. My secretary screens them and she gives me a priority call on things that I absolutely have to answer and if I don't answer them that day she gets after me the next day', Jim told us. 'I never leave the phone on if I'm in meetings. I think it's rude to allow yourself to be interrupted in the middle of meetings. I don't carry my BlackBerry around to meetings in the office. I use it extensively when I'm travelling, but never in the office. And I usually try, when I leave the office, between six and seven at night, not to do very much at home, other than read the paper or magazine articles and things like that, that are interesting.'

In the age of the Internet, many senior executives offer their own weblog – a blog – as a source of communication. At Mitsubishi Corporation, Yorihiko Kojima, the President and CEO, has his own internal blog. Some leaders have found blogs to be a persuasive marketing tool – Jonathan Schwartz, CEO and president of tech giant Sun Microsystems, David Neeleman, founder and CEO of JetBlue Airways, and Richard Edelman, of Edelman, the largest independent PR firm in the world, are all avid corporate bloggers. Among our interviewees, John Brock of Coca-Cola had started his own internal blog – 'It has proven to be a great way of informally communicating with people.'

In his blog, Jonathan Schwartz, says: 'We've moved from the information age to the participation age, and trust is the currency of the participation age. Companies need to speak with one voice and be authentic. Blogging allows you to speak out authentically on your own behalf, and in the long run people will recognise that. Do it consistently and they trust you.'

Studies show that 45 per cent of Fortune 1000 executives think that corporate blogs are growing in credibility as a way to develop and build brands. 'For corporations, the attractions of corporate blogging are varied, but include improving market status, personalising customer relationships, boosting public relations and improving recruitment. Corporate blogs are also being used to foster internal collaboration and improve knowledge management. One of the key benefits of corporate blogging is that companies can track thousands of posts and know what Internet users are thinking about in real time', says Jose Esteves of Spain's IE Business School and an expert on corporate blogging. 'For researchers, like me, it also offers a new mirror to see into the corporate soul.'

Expect to be misunderstood

The best leaders have an innate ability to identify what needs to be done today and what can wait. They know the key messages to communicate from day to day, from audience to audience. They prioritise constantly, aware that wars are lost by fighting on too many fronts. This requires a high degree of patience. 'Everyone feels we're moving like a bullet', one leader confided. 'But I feel like we're crawling.' Pace is relative.

Communication demands patience. It is surprising how easily you can be misunderstood – and for us it's not an English language problem, it is a question of understanding, emphasis and expression. We had a communication go out in the organisation, and in Europe we went to three different countries, and they said, 'Hey, Kevin, this is great. We get it; we understand you're growing, you're not shrinking the business, but you're going into new businesses, et cetera.' And then we came back to America, same communication, and my colleagues in America said, 'Kevin, what the hell are you doing? You're shrinking our business.'

Leaders learn to modify how they speak, to make their vocabulary more simple and easy, in an attempt to get their message understood. The reality is that each person reads material from their own perspective, taking their own meaning from what is written, and you need to try to predict that. That goes for both emails and spoken word.

The reality is that leaders want to do the right thing and communicate and be clear and transparent but have to spend so much time checking that the communication isn't possibly going to be misinterpreted, or misunderstood, by great sections of the organisation that sometimes the timing is not as swift as they want it to be. And guess what? After all that, it still gets read the wrong way.

This is yet another reason why all good communicators share one underlying quality: strong self-esteem. Only when strongly grounded can leaders listen twice as much as they speak and when they speak it is the truth.

Resources

Judi Bevan, *The Rise and Fall of Marks & Spencer . . . and How It Rose Again*, Profile, 2007

Phyllis Mindell, *How to Say it For Executives*, Prentice Hall, 2005

4 Navigating a new route

'Clients come first. Relationships are tougher, pricing is hard, issues are more intense, companies are struggling, so I spend a lot of time with clients. You've got to leverage yourself deeper into the organisation, use the skills of all your people, and use the processes you built in good times to cover the tough times.'

Sam DiPiazza, PwC

Crisis *and* opportunity

'It is vital to see this challenge as an opportunity, to boldly face up to it, and to continue to provide value to customers', says Kazuyasu Kato of Kirin Holdings. Tom Glocer phrases it differently though his sentiments are much the same: 'Terrible markets are a great time to extend the amount of open water you have on the competition.'

Or take this view from Ed Dolman of Christie's International: 'Over the last few months, despite the obvious disappointment at suddenly seeing revenues falling and remuneration levels being reduced, and going through a lot of the painful aspects of downsizing the business and letting people go, there is a real feeling that we've got an opportunity to take back the company, shape it to how we want it to look for the next two, three years, that there's much more control being applied, and that we've got much more control in this market. There's a more stable working environment, people are basically much happier with their lot. There's less poaching going on, they're glad to be employed. It's a totally different environment to manage in, and it does mean that you feel empowered to influence some of the changes that you've been trying to make over the last two or three years but just haven't been able to put in place because of all the other pressures of growing the business and hanging on to your top staff.'

In the crisis is the opportunity. Time after time people told us that the crisis – any crisis – had to be viewed as an opportunity, an opportunity to learn, an opportunity to change, an opportunity to restructure, an opportunity to change personnel, but always an opportunity.

'In the company we've developed a slogan that while everybody's suffering in this crisis we should also think through what opportunities there might be in this crisis. The Chinese word for crisis is made up of two characters. The first character is *wei*. Wei means danger. And the second is *ji* which means opportunity', says Victor Fung. 'While we are suffering from the dangers and the problems we should not lose sight of the fact that this also allows us a lot of opportunity. And that's the way we have approached this crisis. While we're trying to minimise the impact of the adverse side we're constantly saying, how can we emerge from this crisis stronger than we went in? How can we improve our market position?'

If a crisis is a balance between danger and opportunity then the challenges posed to leaders in this situation are also often paired and balanced. Such qualities as openness and decisiveness as well as the need for decisive analytic rigour coupled with active listening to both the ideas and the emotional concerns of people, tests the mettle of a leader very profoundly.

This was particularly brought home talking with Carlos Fernandez, chairman and CEO of the Mexican brewer Modelo (whose brands include the beer Corona). Carlos began working for Grupo Modelo at 13 and was just 29 when he succeeded his uncle Don Antonio Fernandez as CEO in 1997. He is a member of a five-family trust which owns the controlling interest in the brewery.

'Without any question, last year was a difficult one. This one is not going to be any easier, but I'm convinced that a crisis opens doors to new opportunities. For instance, we're working on increasing our presence in Mexico and international markets, to strengthen our previous platform, and to focus on being more competitive', Carlos told us.

We pushed Carlos on what Modelo actually does to make this happen. He highlighted six elements to seizing the opportunities presented by the crisis.

Long-term vision: 'We don't execute or do anything on just a short-term action. We have clear goals.'

Concentrate on what you are good at: 'We focus on what we know best, and that's really beer and how to manage a brewery. We focus on the market, the way we take our products to the market, how we deliver our products to clients, how we make sure the client is convinced of our product's potential and will drink it.'

Build management systems to weather the storm: 'What we have to do now is to minimise any negative impact and to create the best management systems that we can with our teams, to respond to any unforeseen events.'

The adaptive will survive: 'We are used to adjusting many of our expectations, we are prepared to reposition our cost structure, we know how to build products in an environment where there is a lack of purchasing power, so we can work out pricing and changes in demand. We are prepared to confront it.'

Hold firm: 'Turbulent times, yes, but I would say that it really has not changed. We have to pursue a steady profit and excellence in quality in what we produce and the services we offer. We also have to be better aligned. Working together we can chart our own course or direction. We are flexible. Every day we define our destiny in some way, but by maintaining what has made us successful, maintaining our traditions, and always keeping in mind that change is the only constant.'

Be positive: 'I'm trying to see in these events possibilities of a better future and a better performance for everyone. I try every day to convince and to make everyone understand that we continue to be a very strong company, and that we have a long-term vision, that 80 years of history has not been only about good times. There have also been bad times, challenging times, and we have the tools and flexibility needed to face this change in the way we lead.'

There is not much you can argue with here, but we like to think of navigating a new route forward as a process of understanding a series of balances. The first of these is the fact that a crisis always presents opportunities. The second is that thinking about what's best has to work hand in hand with taking action. Leaders need to think *and* act.

Think *and* act

'Management is all about execution in the marketplace, and we've got to do that more flawlessly and more precisely than ever before. That's everything from visual inventory to cases on display, to advertising, local marketing in combination with cases on display to try to drive profitable growth', says John Brock of Coca-Cola Enterprises.

Leadership is a balancing act. In turbulent times this is even more apparent. The balance must be struck between thinking and action. Do you need to act now or can you make a more considered response at a later date? Do you have everyone onside before you make a move? Make no mistake, in a crisis immediate responses with no thought to their future implications are tempting. After all, execution is how leaders are measured. We all want to do something. People are desperate for action in the face of a crisis, but action needs to be combined with thoughtfulness. Action for its own sake is rarely a good thing.

Yet execution is central to any leadership role. Sometimes companies and their leaders need to hold their breath and just jump. There can be no going back. Executing on a plan is often preferable to cogitating about potential new plans or changing the plan halfway through.

'There is no plan B', confessed Stuart Rose of Marks & Spencer when we spoke to him. 'I remember telling the chairman in quite the same way about this, saying, "Well, look, if I can't fix the business don't ask me if I have an alternative plan. I haven't got one. I've only got one plan and we're just going to keep going at this, guys, until either I get sacked or I'm proved right. There ain't no turning, we're not moving left or right. That's the way, that's going to pay off and I won't change the plan now." '

Leaders learn the need to separate what is urgent from what is important; and that comes down to judgement. The leaders who fail are those who micromanage and overcomplicate everything; those leaders who are convinced they must be involved in every detail. Leaders tend to be curious about everything but the effective ones realise they cannot be an expert in every single area of their business and they have to rely on the expertise of others. If you have the right people in place then this is not hard because you trust those people to tell you what is crucial; and they grow and develop because they know they have your support – we all know how good it feels to be relied on.

The think/act balance is at the heart of what we are often looking for when we come to recruit a leader. They need to be action-oriented but also strategic. 'The ideal person is someone who has a successful and demonstrable record in doing and planning; someone who has a proven record with experience in running profit centres, staff support functions and, especially, the strategic planning function within a corporation. Now, if you have somebody that can strategise and execute and you've got a record that they have done it successfully, then you're home', says Gerry Roche, senior chairman of Heidrick & Struggles.

Hard *and* soft

Tom Glocer joined the Reuters Group in 1993 as vice president and deputy counsel of Reuters America. He held a number of senior leadership positions before being named CEO of Reuters Group in July 2001. In April 2008, Reuters was acquired by Thomson, and he continued as CEO of the combined group.

'I had an unusual formative experience. I took over essentially a couple of weeks before 9/11 in what was then considered a pretty bad financial services recession and assumed leadership of a company that had come as close as it could to laying down and dying after 150 years. But this meant I had great freedom in what I could do. I made a lot of mistakes, but could cut pretty strongly and kill the old culture to start a new one.

'Now, it's a different exercise because it's a much healthier patient altogether, but the change we're driving is: What's the new company? What does it stand for? What's the mission? What are the values? What do we want the culture to be? I have probably spent much more time on the soft side of things than the more hard-edged ones. All the nitty-gritty stuff's getting done – we did 10,000 office moves last year – but I am essentially a new CEO with the opportunity to re-set the goals of the company.'

There is a need for balance at every turn as you contemplate navigating a new route forward. One of the most significant themes which came across as we travelled the world talking to leaders was the need to combine the hard and the soft sides of business. At times this appears to be an impossibly difficult balancing act.

To mix our body parts, the knee-jerk assumption is that turbulent times require hard balled decisions, a relentless eye on costs, redundancies, cash flow above all. The leaders we talked to were happy to make difficult decisions, but their emphasis was on the human side of their businesses, the so-called soft side. Yes, you need to manage cash. Yes, you need to keep a lid on costs. But you also need to manage, guide, inspire and lead people.

Everyone is in a people business. 'Largely it's about people, finding the right people, putting them in the right place, having a shared vision, providing them with support – probably limited in the current circumstances – and then moving forward and seeing the results', Alexey Mordashov of Severstal confided.

The stereotypical instant response of companies in a crisis is to slash human resources and marketing budgets. The leaders we interviewed had little time for such simple reactions. Indeed, time after time we encountered companies which had actually ramped up their training and development activities.

Again, this is something K.V. Kamath was insistent on. 'We do about ten days of training for every single employee in the organisation, and I proudly tell my team that I take 10 days off every year to train myself.

It could be just sitting at the feet of somebody who is well regarded and listening to him speak and discuss, or engaging with a person, it could be a CEO forum, it could be any other type of activity where you are listening to others and their experiences and building on your knowledge, or it could be things that are not really day-to-day things. Technology for example, understanding new technology and the way it has played out.'

'We are doing massive re-training during this crisis inside the company. This helps to give meaning to this both at the company and at the individual employee level', says Victor Fung. 'At a later stage we will go against the grain. When everybody's cutting back their hiring we will be selectively hiring, and I'm sure we'll get the cream of the crop. We will emerge stronger out of this crisis.'

Cutting numbers *and* still recruiting great people appears contradictory. But a company cannot simply say no to talent. 'The bold companies are going to go ahead and do recruiting anyway and then figure out a different way to cut costs and they will have a competitive advantage down the line', predicts Bijan Khosrowshahi, formerly of Fuji Fire and Marine.

IQ *and* EQ

Another balance which needs to be struck is between IQ and EQ (emotional quotient), smartness and sensitivity. Forget about the heroic or macho leader marching troops blindly forward. Leadership requires sensitivity.

Daniel Goleman's book *Primal Leadership* makes the case for cultivating emotionally intelligent leaders. In it, Goleman and co-authors Richard E. Boyatzis and Annie McKee explore how the four domains of emotional intelligence – self-awareness, self-management, social awareness and relationship management – give rise to different styles of leadership. These constitute a leadership repertoire, which enlightened leaders can master to maximise their effectiveness.

Our belief is that, at the heart of any top job and integral to leadership is the ability to balance IQ and EQ. Leaders now require a broad spectrum of knowledge. The best leaders are adept at applying their analytical skills and their emotional skills at the right times. They aren't purely people people, but can make sense of complex market data and strategic plans. The important thing is that they are able to balance the two elements.

This balance requires a strong equilibrium within oneself. We have referred to the central role self-esteem plays in a leader's effectiveness. Genuine self-esteem translates into decision making that is not full of rationalisations or defensiveness. It is open to other perspectives and to many streams of data, but still manages to be clear and decisive.

Another leader we talked to put it like this: 'The problem is that you think that everyone thinks like you. But if they thought like you, they wouldn't need you as their leader.'

Today *and* tomorrow

'I've got a 55 per cent long-term strategic shareholder who doesn't manage quarter by quarter', says Tom Glocer of Thomson Reuters, 'but we certainly keep score quarterly and even monthly.' He continues, 'You can convince yourself a lot of stupid things are really long-term strategic and they're not, but we have a sensible balance. Our shareholders know that the planning horizon is not necessarily quarter by quarter. We would never go out and buy a big credit company to smooth our earnings quarter to quarter.'

At PwC, to make sense of the crisis one of the reactions was to put some of the company's best minds to work on the future. At its busiest time of year, it took some of its brightest partners and put together a team to look at how the changes underway were likely to affect business in three to five years. 'Our view is that the world has structurally changed, for at least the next decade', says Sam DiPiazza. 'US growth is going to slow, capital is going to be more expensive, regulatory environments are going to be tougher, and it will be more difficult to cross borders. Some businesses are better prepared than others, but unless we actually apply all that to our own business model, we'll miss that change, and so we're deep into that right now.'

One of the big questions we asked people is how you manage in the short term bearing in mind long-term opportunities. For the CEOs of public companies this is particularly difficult, because of the quarter-to-quarter scrutiny that they're under. This revealed another paradox: the balance between dealing with the nitty-gritty of the moment – dramatic changes in the marketplace and so on – and an ability to keep an eye on the long-term prize.

Says K.V. Kamath: 'You have to have the ability to stand up and say what we are doing is for the long term, we will try to do what is good in the short term, but we will work with the long-term context. There are headwinds, but they do not stay there all the time. You have to plan on blue skies. Businesses you have built have to be nurtured. If you are building for the short term you can chop and change every now and then, but if you are building for the long term you stay the course and then you reassess.'

No matter what the circumstances, change begins with a vision. It has to. 'You cannot make a change or even engage in a process of change if at the beginning you do not know where you want to go. Establishing the destination, establishing the purpose is fundamental. If you do not have a purpose, do not even try to make any changes, because they will fail. Having from the beginning a clear vision, a clear sense of purpose, is fundamental to any change', Carlos Ghosn told us. 'Up to 1999, Nissan was a company in disarray. Company objectives were set and people worked hard to achieve them, but then the course kept changing. People lost a sense of motivation and did not know where to go. When I came on board in 1999, my sole objective was very simple: it was to revive Nissan. This objective would determine all our priorities. It would determine even the people we would count on to achieve them. In 1999, we had to revive the company. There would be no compromises and no half measures. Nothing that could threaten the revival of the company would be accepted.

'What was true then is still true today. If you do not have a shared and attractive destination, you can forget about any process of change.'

The big picture does not disappear just because the immediate reality is so daunting. It cannot. A leader and an organisation without a future is going nowhere.

This was repeatedly brought home to us in our interviews. We found that leaders were fire fighting, but they were also insisting that here was an opportunity to re-calibrate future aspirations, plans and visions. The best leaders have a constant sense of the future they want to create.

'I try to keep a part of my agenda dedicated to strategic, important and not urgent topics', says Alexey Mordashov of Severstal. He is a passionate reader of Jim Collins' books, which inspired him, in November 2007, to set up a 'hedgehog committee' made up of the top ten managers of the group to discuss long-term strategy. For the uninitiated, a hedgehog concept is explained by Collins as a frame of reference for decisions, an understanding of what you are best at. The metaphor behind it is that a fox wants to eat a hedgehog and has a variety of cunning ways of springing a surprise. Every time it happens, the hedgehog has a tried and tested response: to curl into a prickly ball. It is simple and it works. The challenge is to find your own hedgehog concept, the strategy or way of working which makes you the best in the world or resilient in the face of a competitive fox.

'What the hedgehog concept means for us is long-term competitiveness. And these discussions helped us to develop a shared vision about the company says Alexey Mordashov.

Whether they think in hedgehog terms or not, the crisis provides an opportunity to view the world and all of your activities in a sharper focus. This was brought home talking to Tom Glocer of Thomson Reuters. 'What we've done is basically say let's kill all the obvious nice-to-haves out there. Let's use this as an excuse to really do the tougher things that in fatter markets you just don't do, let's actually increase our investment in the two or three things that we think really make a difference', says Glocer. 'The data I've seen suggests that at least over the last two recessions firms that continued to both invest organically and in acquisition significantly out-performed their peers when the economy eventually recovered because the natural thing that everyone does is cut, cut, cut and I'm not convinced that's the right thing.'

In a crisis a price is often paid in human and financial terms, but the best leaders always have their eyes on the future prize.

Common sense *and* complexity

We asked Tom Glocer about how he had changed his time management since the going became even more turbulent. 'I've spent a bit more time on safety factors – making sure our balance sheet is strong, making sure that the credit facility is truly a committed one and not a facility in name, a bit more idiot-proofing because safety first has got to be the right approach; focusing on cash and liquidity and we re-financed our debt even though it really wasn't due for another 18 months because I've always had the belief that you borrow money when you don't need it because when you do it's often not available. Now, that just turned out to be lucky. We hit a good window, but we took out our average maturity to something like six, seven years and don't have any real debt coming due. Now, would we have done that in a normal market? Maybe, but we're just a little bit more focused on that sort of thing.'

Some see the downturn as a wake-up call, a reminder of the eternal verities of the business world. 'In turbulent times, an enterprise has to be managed both to withstand sudden blows and to avail itself of sudden unexpected opportunities. This means that in turbulent times the fundamentals have to be managed, and managed well', wrote Peter Drucker.[1]

Here, too, balance has to be struck between commonsensical commercial realities and the complexities of a global downturn.

Says Ed Dolman of Christie's: 'I think it has reminded everybody to go back to common-sense management, to really go back to having faith in what you believe. Everybody's faith in anybody who tries to sit in front of you and predict what may be happening in two months, three months, a week has completely disintegrated. If you look back and listen to the protestations and advice given by financial advisers, pension actuaries, marketers, even other businesses, you realise that actually it all amounts to a hill of beans. My takeaway from all this is that actually there are some very simple basics on which our economies and every business depends, and no matter how clever

1 Peter Drucker, *Managing in Turbulent Times*, HarperCollins, 1980.

you try to be, you can't really escape from that. As a CEO I'm much less influenced now by proposals to seek profit and growth through complicated and sometimes overly optimistic models. I rely much more on my gut instinct and common sense now to guide me, and I'm much less secure in accepting the advice of outside advisers.'

There was a confident sense of certainty to much of what they said. We asked Kazuyasu Kato of Kirin Holdings how he believed Kirin would weather the storm. 'We will shift the focus of group management from quantitative expansion to qualitative expansion and pursue a comprehensive beverage group strategy by ensuring: a good balance between domestic and overseas business; a healthy balance between our main businesses of alcohol, soft drinks/foods, and pharmaceuticals; stable cash flow; and a business portfolio that can create synergies.'

One leader we talked to envisioned a dashboard in front of him with a set of instruments asking basic business questions: do you have capital; do you have liquidity; do you have the right products; do you have the people; do you have the processes? 'If you have all these things and they are showing a full tank or near full tank, I think you can say we can probably last this out and proceed on that basis. But if you find any of those dashboard instruments running short, then you need to look at what it is that you need to top up', he explained.

Humility *and* strength

We were struck also by the balance between humility and strength. The leaders we encountered have egos and a generous measure of self-confidence. They are all successful and in powerful positions influencing large organisations and the well-being and livelihoods of thousands of people – sometimes hundreds of thousands. But, there was never a hint of complacency and all saw their organisation as a team. Typical was this comment from Nick Stephan, CEO of Phoenix Partners: 'The bottom line is we have a great crew. I attribute the bulk of our success to my partners frankly. They are amazing at what they do, be it broking, be it finding talented brokers, or cultivating relationships. Also just the depth of their rolodex. It's really off the back of doing a lot of recruiting of friends and of friends of friends and down that path, where it's someone you know. And someone's putting them forward, someone's vouching for them.'

Ed Dolman of Christie's International had an interesting take on the mix of personalities in his team: 'I've always had a team around me that's got a balance. I have hawks and I have doves. I have dreamers and I have people who are fantastically rational. For the last three or four years it's been the aspirational dreamers within the business who have been probably the loudest voices and their decision making has been vindicated through growth and profitability. And now in my team the hawks, the rational people, the guys who've always got their feet on the ground, the defence line, are now much more to the fore. There's been a big shift from the revenue-generating, aspirational, creative side of the team to the very functional, feet-on-the-ground realists, who are rolling their sleeves up and getting stuck in. Strength comes from having diversity in your management team. Different people can play more or less active roles, depending on what the business demands are.'

Humility outperforms charisma. Humility is based on genuine self-esteem not tiny grandiosity. In his book *Good to Great*, Jim Collins examines how a good company becomes an exceptional company. The book introduces a new term to the leadership lexicon: Level 5 leadership. Level 5 refers to the highest level in a hierarchy of executive capabilities. Leaders at the other four levels may be successful but they are unable to elevate companies from mediocrity to sustained excellence.

Level 5 leadership challenges the assumption that transforming companies from good to great requires larger-than-life leaders. The leaders that came out on top in Collins's five-year study were relatively unknown outside their industries. The findings appear to signal a shift of emphasis away from the hero to the anti-hero. According to Collins, humility is a key ingredient of Level 5 leadership. His simple formula is Humility + Will = Level 5. 'The central dimension for Level 5 is a leader who is ambitious first and foremost for the cause, for the company, for the work, not for himself or herself; and has an absolutely terrifying iron will to make good on that ambition', says Collins. 'It is that combination, the fact that it's not about them, it's not first and foremost for them, it's for the company and its long-term interests, of which they are just a part. But it's not a meekness; it's not a weakness; it's not a wallflower type. It's the other side of the coin.'

Good mentors not only have solid self-esteem themselves but they are also able to realistically mirror the strengths and needs of their team members in a way that builds self-esteem throughout the team and ultimately the organisation.

Navigating a new route forward is, as we have seen, an incredibly difficult balancing act. Sam DiPiazza of PwC provided a pithy summary of what needs to happen: 'Don't change your dream, adjust it to a new reality.'

Resources

Jim Collins, *Good to Great,* Collins, 2004

Jim Collins, *How the Mighty Fall,* Collins, 2009

Peter Drucker, *Managing in Turbulent Times,* Harper Collins, 1980

Daniel Goleman, Richard Boyatzis, and Annie McKee, *Primal Leadership*, Harvard Press, 2004

5 Mastering mutinies

'The bigger the company is, the more the job is really managing the people, putting the right people at the right place, thinking about the future of the company, trying to bring everything under one roof, setting the strategy.'

Monika Ribar CEO of Panalpina

Horses for courses[1]

A young manager had a highly delegative management style. He delegated as much as he could and took great pride in doing so. Then a crisis arose and he needed things done and done in a hurry. He became more authoritative – we need to do this, we need to do that, I need you to do this by Friday, he told people. Did they rally to his flag? Did they appreciate that his formerly easy-going management style was a luxury the organisation could ill afford at that precise moment? No, of course not. The result was a complete backlash. His staff rapidly reached the point of rebellion.

Puzzled by this, the manager went to his boss and explained that his staff were mutinous and emotionally

1 Thank you to George Halvorson of Kaiser Permanente for this story.

distraught. His leadership was simply not working, he confessed.

His boss was a highly experienced leader, one of those managerial sages you come across – hopefully early on in your career. 'The problem is you've got winter horses', he said straightaway. 'What's a winter horse?' asked the confused manager.

The boss had grown up on a farm on the Minnesota, South Dakota border. He explained that on the farm they had some riding horses, which they would ride during the summer. Then, in the autumn, they would put them in the barn to protect them from the freezing temperatures of winter. Come spring, when they wanted to ride the horses again, they put the saddles on and the horses would buck them off. They would have to re-break the horses every spring.

To solve the problem and avoid the long-drawn-out process of breaking the horses in every year, they changed the process. At least once a month throughout the winter they went into each stall, put a saddle on the horse and then rode it around the barn, or in some cases, led the horse around the barn to get it used to the saddle. By spring, the horses were comfortable with saddles and being ridden.

'What you have here are winter horses', explained the boss, patiently. 'You've delegated so completely that they have no sense at all that there's a hierarchy. They have no sense that it's a really good idea – good for everybody – for them to be doing team-like things with you to get through this crisis. They're resisting you emotionally and probably don't even know why. They're just bucking you off because you haven't done that kind of thing for a while. I recommend that what you do is meet with them at least once every month, but probably every week, to go through things as a group. Spend some time monitoring more closely what they're doing and getting involved more directly in the management of their process. Not to micromanage them, but just to keep the emotional context in place that says that there is a hierarchy and that they're in it.'

Unused to being told what to do, with no memory of previous recessions, there are a lot of winter horses out there. It is the leader's job to understand them and to get them onside and extract great performances from them.

People first

Leading in turbulent times is firstly about getting people behind you. (Really it all comes down to people, doesn't it?) If you are dealing with any sort of change then how you manage people is critical. What is amazing is that we study business at university or business school and spend 95 per cent of the time learning about strategy, marketing, corporate finance, organisational structures and the rest, and about 5 per cent on people skills. Yet when we finish our studies and start working we immediately find the ratio is exactly the inverse. Personnel issues fill the days, whether you're working in an organisation of 10 or 10,000. Day to day, every plan you make and every strategy you devise revolves around having the right people in place.

There are three key factors that keep employees happy, engaged and loyal to the company. These constitute the underlying objectives in everything that leaders do. They are:

1. Interest in what they do – be it marketing, finance, consulting, or whatever.
2. Compensation – not just what people are paid and their bonuses but treating people fairly.
3. Learning – when candidates approach us as a search firm it is usually because they feel they have stopped learning and developing in their current firm.

Increasingly, as we look for the leaders of the future we find ourselves coming back to that third point – learning – as the most critical. Generation Y – those born between 1977 and 2005 – will have had an average of 14 jobs by the time they are 38. It seems to us that the organisations that are going to succeed in the long term are those that provide their employees with the right learning opportunities. When we are promoting people or looking for future leaders, we always look closely at how they encourage, develop and train the talent below them. There are few more effective tests of leadership potential.

Follow folly

Any leader is only as good as their followers. We heard a story about the founder of an international chain of hotels. His measure of success was whether the maid cleaning a room in one of the chain's furthest outposts would neatly turn up the toilet paper. It is a very small thing to consider in a huge international operation, but it is built around realising that if the leader is doing their job well then it is having an impact on everyone in the organisation.

When we spoke with H. Patrick Swygert, he was president of Howard University, a job he held from 1995 until June 2008. Patrick studied law at Howard and was previously president at the University of Albany. Along the way, he has taught throughout the world and is on the board of Fannie Mae, United Technologies, the Hartford Financial Services Group and is on the CIA's External Advisory Board.

'You can be a great leader, or at least have the attributes of a great leader, and have no followers', Patrick observed. 'How often have we seen people who, at least on paper, fit the profile, but they just can't get people to work and walk with them. I would say that comes about for two reasons. One, some believe they can act without the advice or input of others. They believe they know everything or know as much, or more, than anyone in the room. They tend to only half listen and people pick up on that very, very quickly.

'Second, there are some people who don't have that kind of all-encompassing, far-reaching intelligence; they're intelligent in one way, but not intelligent enough to let other people have something to say, and a piece of the outcome. I think that's one of the reasons why some, otherwise brilliant, people can't do anything but lead themselves to the rest rooms.' (On a similar theme, one amazed new leader told us, 'People do actually follow you to the bathroom!')

Strike quickly

None of this should suggest that managing people is easy. It isn't. But to avoid mutinous outbreaks any crisis must first be thought of in human terms. Business is human. For the leaders we talked to this was automatically understood. You don't – usually – get to lead a large organisation unless you are good at the people side of business.

'This is a time when the true values of an organisation surface and I think leaders have to be very careful not to play favourites and not to send mixed messages. If you've got a prima donna out there, the way you treat that prima donna could undermine everything else you want to do. So, first you've got to engage that prima donna and make them part of the solution, not part of the problem. If they refuse to become part of the solution, you've got a tough call, because if you vary from your values your organisation may not come out of this anywhere close to its potential', says PwC's Sam DiPiazza. 'We're a partnership and we have our share of difficult people, but we also have a long history of saying, you don't win as a star, you win as a member of a team. In professional services everything filters right through the organisation like it's fibre optics.'

The second element in ensuring that mutinous thoughts were kept to a minimum was seizing the initiative immediately. A lot of the leaders we talked to jump-started organisational momentum as soon as they possibly could.

A great example of this approach comes from Henry Fernandez. 'When the crisis hit, we immediately put into effect, in the first two to three months, a variety of programmes completely attacking the business as usual environment. A lot of the programmes had nothing to do with the fact that we were dealing with a crisis. They were my pet projects, what I wanted to change was harder to do in a normal environment.

'I said to people, we have less resources than we did a year ago, but we still want to do a lot of things, so let's go out and talk to other players in the industry to see what they have that we don't that will be beneficial to incorporate in our business as opposed to inventing it here. People were very open to it and a year ago they were fighting me tooth and nail.

'The key to change and dealing with resistors has been to take that force, really mould it and put it behind us to make it a positive as opposed to a negative force. So, the majority of the company has been significantly more open to change than was possible a year ago. The people who have resisted change have been ganged up on by the others who feel that their viability, their income, their bonus is at stake if everyone doesn't run in the right direction. It has been positive. There is a crisis, you've got to monopolise it, you've got to take it, you've got to put it to work for you and that's what we've done.'

This gets things started. Next come some even trickier issues. As Fernandez explains: 'The harder question, which we're now focused on, is have you spent enough time looking beyond the crisis to what the industry will look like? Can you make some assumptions of what the industry will look like, based on what you know today?

It's hard. A lot of people don't want to deal with it. They want to deal with the day-to-day. They're tired. They're stressed out. The free time that they have, they want to go and relax and get a drink and escape as opposed to thinking about business and things like this.

'I tell people, go home and don't talk about this. Try not to read the paper. Go to the park and play frisbee. Take your vacation, go and relax. No one is allowed not to take their vacation. Second, keep an optimistic perspective. We have a great business. We have cash in the balance sheet. We're not going out of business. The only thing is how do we profit from this? So, it's not a negative. We're not covering the downside. We need to focus on covering the upside. That gets people optimistic and in high spirits.

'We also have an advisory board that is composed of 15 to 20 of the who's who of the investment world. I told them at the last meeting that when we next meet I don't want to hear about this crisis anymore. I don't want to hear about what happened, what didn't happen, the factors involved. We don't want to hear any of that stuff. We want to focus on what will the investment industry look like after the crisis.'

Rose on retail

One of the best examples of handling a crisis we have encountered was the story of Sir Stuart Rose. After working for the UK retailer Marks & Spencer (M&S), Rose worked for the Burton Group, Argos, Booker and Arcadia. As his career had taken off, M&S's fortunes had declined.

In May 2004, it was announced that M&S's chairman, Luc Vandevelde, was departing. Soon after, Stuart Rose had a Thursday morning meeting with non-executive director Kevin Lomax. Little did they know that a few hours later, the retailer Sir Philip Green would launch a hostile takeover for M&S with £8 billion tabled as his offer. Later that evening, M&S approached Stuart Rose and by the following Monday he was installed as the company's CEO. Being in the right place at the right time is as important at the top of the corporate tree as it is anywhere else.

But before the new leader celebrates his or her luck, they need to remember that if everything were perfect the organisation probably wouldn't need a new leader. The new hire – no matter what the job – usually encounters trouble. When Rose took over as CEO at M&S, the once legendary UK retailer was on its knees. To put its problems in perspective, in 1997 M&S was the second largest market capitalised retailer in the world after Wal-Mart; M&S was capitalised at $25 billion and Wal-Mart $60 billion. By 2005/6 M&S was capitalised as the 28th largest retailer, still at $25 billion (having been down to $12 billion), and Wal-Mart was at $300 billion. M&S was saddled with a mountain of inventory – £3 billion-worth. Its clothing range was confusingly branded, with 16 sub-brands. M&S was slow to move with fashion and its clothes looked increasingly dowdy in its cluttered high street stores. Among other problems, consultants were running 31 'strategic projects'.

The good news in such circumstances is that the leader may have nothing to lose. 'Believe it or not, I don't think they saw me as a white knight; I think they saw me as absolute desperation: "Well we are not sure he can do it but he is the last resort, so let's give it a try." I'm not being falsely modest!' says Rose. 'Obviously, if you come into a business that is in a crisis you have the disadvantage that you're coming in at a crisis, but actually you have a bigger advantage – the advantage is that the board frankly would have agreed to anything. I had absolute control, which was key.

'The second thing is that I've been in a few businesses that have been in a bit of trouble in the last 10 years or so and I think what I spotted fairly early on is that it wasn't as if they were careering away in the wrong direction, they just weren't doing anything at all.'

Stuart Rose spent the first weeks and months of his leadership of M&S fighting off Philip Green's unwelcome takeover bid. It was not until July 2004 that the spectre of a takeover was exorcised. Having a clear short-term challenge helped focus energies.

The great thing about a crisis is that action is necessary immediately. There is no time to hatch a complex strategy and then to roll it out through the organisation. A willingness to roll your sleeves up and execute is what the organisation needs. It wasn't so much that the company was continuing to make the wrong decisions. It had made them and was standing amid the results without much idea of what to do next.

This situation was made for Stuart Rose. 'It's a bit like the old stories – people are so desperate for leadership that even if you lead them the wrong way they'd rather go that way than go nowhere at all. People were almost literally standing around saying either, “There isn’t a problem, what problem?” Or, “There is a problem but we don’t know what to do about it.” Some were saying go left and some were saying go right; and the rest, well, it just passed over their heads.’

In such a pressured environment, nearly right now is often better than perfection tomorrow. In a complex and difficult business situation with the press and expectant employees hanging on your every word, the chances of hatching a watertight, perfect strategy are extremely slim. You have to compromise on perfection to execute in accordance with what the company desperately needs. Stuart Rose remembers what he told himself: ‘Be 95 per cent right rather than 100 per cent right; follow your gut instincts; cut back minimally on research; use the benefit of 30 years’ experience; you aren’t going to be right in every respect but mostly you could get it right by touch or feel, and then if you are in any doubt at all about doing something today or doing something tomorrow, do it today.’ Of course, as Rose candidly admits, mistakes are made.

Again the key was the human connection. The sooner you can get people on board the better. ‘I sat down with probably 20 managers in the first week’, says Stuart Rose. ‘I said, “Come in, sit down, you don’t know me” – though one or two of them did remember me from my previous time with the company. I said, “Tell me what you think the problems are in the business. Tell me what you think we should do, tell me how you think we should fix it.” There were those saying, “I’m so glad that somebody like you has come in. You're talking about products, you're talking about prices, you're talking about shopkeeping. You know, if only we could do this, this, this or this." So you put them down as a tick.

'There were others saying, "There's no problem here, absolutely alright, all you need to do is leave us to ourselves and go and do something else because my bit of the company's absolutely fine." And there were those who weren't quite sure what to do. Interestingly enough, they were the most difficult ones because you had to make a very quick decision as to whether you could get them there or was it just going to take you too long. Can you teach this person to swim before the pool fills up, or can't you?'

Tone setting

A final example of stopping mutinies in their tracks by getting people onboard comes from Seung-Yu Kim, who became CEO of the Hana Financial Group in Korea in 1997. The timing was not auspicious. 'Our economy was really in trouble. Our currency was overvalued and in my first 100 days 12 of the 30 biggest Korean conglomerates were bankrupted. The last one was Kia Motors, which we had a big exposure to. It went bankrupt on 20 July. I still remember the date.'

Seung-Yu Kim had been with Hana since the time it had a mere 20 people. Hana developed its commercial banking in the early 1990s and Seung-Yu Kim was well placed because he had prior experience and a network in commercial banking. This did not, however, prepare him for taking over a company at the height of a far-reaching economic crisis. Faced with a crisis, Seung-Yu Kim focused on 'awakening my people', reshaping and restructuring.

From the start he worked at making all employees feel appreciated. After taking over as CEO in February, he led the purchase of a training centre in April. 'At the time we had fewer than 1000 people so every week, in the evening, I met with some of them. In my first 100 days in particular I tried to appreciate them one by one.'

Surrounded by crisis, Seung-Yu Kim increased salaries by a mere 2 per cent in 1997, put his own pay rise on hold and cut costs. 'For example, I took economy class when I had a business trip overseas. Most CEOs travel first class, but this was part of me showing my people how much I appreciated and valued them. My people followed me and trusted me, and that's why we overcame the financial crisis.' When Seung-Yu Kim insisted on flying economy, the airlines, aware of why he was flying economy, used to leave the neighbouring seat vacant.

Seung-Yu Kim was in the habit of heading home at 9 or 10 o'clock at night. On his way home, if he saw any of the bank's branches with their lights on he stopped off and paid a visit. People working extra hours were regularly treated to pizzas courtesy of the CEO. The pizzas came with a message. 'Whenever I made a surprise visit to our branches, I highlighted the significance of our customers. I always tried to tell people that our shareholders could leave us at any time were we not profitable, but our customers would stay with us if we did our best for them. I also reminded them that they didn't need to look for market trends as market demand is nothing but the products and services which customers want us to provide them. They listened to me. And, now, the strong customer/market-oriented philosophy of the early days of Hana Bank has become the core value of the entire group.'

Beyond mutinies

None of this should suggest that people are not sometimes angry, unhappy and plain mutinous. It happens inevitably in any crisis. Overcoming these very natural emotions calls for empathy from the leader – the leader has to be able to put themselves in the shoes of their followers. From empathy must spring action, not action for the sake of it, but action that is based on being positive and forward-thinking. Mutinies tend to be focused on the troubled moment; leadership trumps this by creating an enticing and compelling future.

Resources

John Kotter, *A Sense of Urgency*, Harvard Press, 2008

Bruce Tulgan, *Not Everyone Gets a Trophy: How to Manage Generation Y*, Jossey Bass, 2009

6 Learning to tack

'In the face of this unprecedented challenge, the single most important quality that every CEO, banker, portfolio manager or politician should possess and display is agility.'

Tom Glocer, CEO, Thomson Reuters

Nimble giants

'Agility has been a major theme and a competitive advantage in our company in the last nine months', Henry Fernandez told us when we talked. 'Prior to the financial crisis, our business lent itself to long and studious deliberations given the longer term, steady and subscription nature of our business. By October of 2008, we realised our clients, mainly only asset managers and pension funds globally, were undergoing incredible changes in their purchasing decisions due to the enormous declines in their revenues (asset-based fees dropping substantially in a very short period). Some clients and prospects needed our tools and had money to spend. Others had the demand but did not have any budgets to purchase. The problem was we did not know which was which. Sorting this out within weeks or a few months was a challenge. We needed to act fast. Otherwise our sales would drop precipitously.

'Our sales force was organised to call on clients like a conventional army conducting a conventional war. What was needed were guerrilla marketing tactics and a rapid transformation of the way we called on our 3000 clients and another 3000 prospects in over 60 countries. We also needed to rapidly change our new product delivery schedule by postponing some less urgent ones and accelerating others dealing with risk management.

'We had never really confronted this kind of situation before. We realised we needed speed and to utilise leverage through other firms in order to produce agility and react to the crisis. We also knew others were facing the same issues. Therefore we embarked on a transformation of the way we conducted day-to-day business. We approached investment information providers (Bloomberg and FactSet) and other kinds of intermediaries (custodians and broker dealers) and proposed a series of joint actions for both of us to discover where the demand and the money was among clients and prospects. We developed sales campaigns by bundling products together. We also actually increased prices for certain products to protect margins and reduced prices of other products to generate volume. We blocked out Fridays as cold calling days. And we accelerated our hiring in lower cost, emerging market centres to help us cope with our higher volume of activity but lower revenue growth. These changes were initially hard to implement but as the financial crisis accelerated, our staff realised they needed to change. I also started the theme of 'a crisis is a terrible thing to waste' to help mobilise our staff and rally them to the cause of rapid change.

'We clearly have not been immune to this crisis, but I believe our light-footedness and guerrilla marketing tactics have helped us cushion the negative impact of this downdraft. A lot of what I implemented I had learned as a child watching a conventional army trying to fight a guerrilla war, where the guerrilla forces were much more agile than the regular army. The former won and the latter lost. By October 2008, I realised this could happen to our company and we needed the agility of a rapid and mobile force. Funny how an experience from my childhood has helped us cope with this crisis! Life has many turns and circles.'

Corporate boating

The executive and paper-laden organisations of not so long ago moved at the sedate and considered speed of supertankers. They could turn eventually, but were not designed for swift changes of directions and a nimble turn of corporate foot.

Now, there is a premium on speed and the willingness to change direction as time and opportunities dictate. The agile organisation is no longer a pipe dream but a commercial necessity. 'This crisis will allow a new set of leadership companies to emerge globally', anticipates Victor Fung. The new breed are likely to be agile by instinct and habit.

'In this kind of environment, it is impossible to come up with an accurate mid-range forecast, and inadvisable to fix any strategy around such a forecast. Therefore, I think it is essential for management to take action with speed above all to shorten the PDCA (Plan/Do/Check/Act) cycle,' Kazuyasu Kato of Kirin Holdings told us.

This message was brought home to us particularly in our conversations with Indian business leaders. They display an impressive willingness to change and adapt with the times. As anyone who has visited the country will attest, chaos and turbulence are facts of everyday life in India. It is a tumultuous nation and this breeds certain characteristics – an ease with complexity and change is just one of them.

K.V. Kamath at ICICI provided a particularly persuasive case for agility. KV = speed. Under Kamath the company has introduced what it calls the 90-day rule.

This was something Kamath encountered a decade ago at a seminar in New York. (Lesson one: leaders learn as they go along and learn from a variety of sources – the seminar was nothing to do with banking.) 'We looked at a model where people were describing how people in Silicon Valley, typically start-ups, would in a very short period of time bring a product to market', Kamath remembers. 'Somebody used a phrase – the 90-day rule – how you brought something from concept to market in 90 days. At the time we were implementing a lot of projects and which were typically two years in length. We thought why not change it to 90 days, why not re-examine what it would take to do it in 90 days and then push it through?'

K.V. Kamath combines urgency with bold and positive thinking: 'We have painted a fourth horizon of growth which we will execute in the coming years. A total of

600 million people in India are unbanked. So, we call it bank the unbanked. That strategy is being slowly worked on. Each strategy has a cost, initially it is looked at as an overhead or something that is not contributing, but in the course of time the market gets excited about it and starts rewarding you. So that is how we have been looking at the market, and trying to deliver – I would say – to the best of our abilities.' Again, turbulent times call for agile organisations and agile minds. K.V.'s brilliantly simple and commercially smart leap is to identify a vast new marketplace.

This is the strategic equivalent of a moon-shot – what Jim Collins called a 'big hairy audacious goal'. Such targets are immensely attractive and persuasive – even when times are tough. It also echoes Chan Kim's and Renée Mauborgne's notion of 'blue ocean strategy'. In their eyes companies need to focus not on the competitor-filled red oceans but on creating their own blue oceans.

Old dog, new tricks

One organisation which has worked hard at making itself more agile is PricewaterhouseCoopers. 'We have made a conscious effort to create a much more collaborative structure in our organisation', Sam DiPiazza told us. Getting 8000 partners on board is a challenging task. But when they were asked about a new decision-making structure which puts greater emphasis on teams rather than individuals, the PwC partners were overwhelmingly in favour – 96 per cent voted for the changes.

Says DiPiazza: 'We took that partner vote right in the middle of the Fannie Mae, Freddie Mac and Lehman collapses. So when we got into October 2008, and saw our clients were struggling around the world, we were able to build responses faster and were more aligned than before. It wasn't a hierarchical top-down response, it was a shared collaborative response – a different model of leadership.'

Sam DiPiazza also referenced the Charles Darwin quote that we included right at the start of this book about the fact that it is not the strongest species that survive, but the one that can most adapt to change. He continued: 'Sometimes, our desire to be collaborative has been an issue to our agility. You have to do both, seek input, listen and then move with the changing environment. When we did our merger 11 years ago, we were operating in a huge boom period. Then the market collapsed and we were slow to move not because we did not see it coming but because we were not agile enough to change. It hurt our performance. This time we were ready and also willing to make decisions quickly.

'Being agile suggests that you always know the right answer and only need to create momentum for change in the organisation. All leaders know that "the right answer" is not always so obvious. But a great leader knows when to call the question, when to make a move. Even if all the facts are not known – something that is often the case.

'A great leader has prepared his or her organisation for the change even before it comes.'

The agile Infosys

As an exemplar of the agile organisation, India's Infosys takes some beating. We talked with Kris Gopalakrishnan, the company's CEO and one of the seven founders of the global consulting and IT services company. Kris became CEO in June 2007 having set up the business in 1981 – a brave decision when most ambitious Indians were pursuing their careers by leaving the country.

'Everything is instantaneous. In fact there are a few things that are different today from the way they were before. One is the speed at which you need to get things done', he observes.

The first thing you notice when you visit is that Infosys is a very young organisation. The average age of its employees is 26 or 27. During the dot-com bubble burst of 2001 Infosys had around 10,000 employees; now it has more than 100,000 employees. 'For almost all of them this is the first downturn. They have been used to a compounded annual growth rate of 35 per cent, fast-track promotions, increments every year. Now, the world has changed', reflects Gopalakrishnan.

Infosys is a great example of what Tom Peters and Robert Waterman labelled 'simultaneous loose–tight properties' in their book *In Search of Excellence*. It manages to combine business discipline with freedom of thought and action. This is corporate nirvana, what has been more recently labelled the 'ambidextrous organisation'.

'The company is very tightly controlled and managed in spite of the size of the organisation. There is a lot of focus on minimising expenses every day, day in and day out. We had already set in place a rhythm of how we manage the business. We had built all that before, so we could react fast, but we still had to overcommunicate to employees and explain to them the situation, where we are and how we are going to face the future. It puts us in a good position. We have almost US$2 billion of cash. We are growing and highly profitable. There are a lot of positives, but of course the longer the situation lasts, the more it will affect us, because our clients are affected, and we have to explain that to our people. We have to become slightly cautious in our approach to how we run the business and what investments we make in the business. We have to reduce the number of initiatives we are taking for the future and things like that', says Kris Gopalakrishnan. 'We do not manage the company by looking at share markets or stock price. We do not worry about that. We say let us look at revenue, margins, cash flow, growth. Those are the things we can influence. Share price is what the market decides.'

We explored with Kris how Infosys is actually managed in practice. We learned from him that Infosys creates themes around each of its strategic initiatives. Around 300 people have been identified as tier one leaders. Then it has a number of department heads and an executive committee. Infosys assigns teams to each of the strategic themes under a programme managed by a central team called Corporate Planning. Kris reviews this periodically and once a quarter there is a detailed review. For the leaders of each of these teams part of their bonus plan is linked to how well the strategy is implemented. As part of the measures to determine the bonus Infosys includes action on strategies.

'They see that the strategy is created as a team exercise. They participated in creating the strategy, they own that and they get to lead it. They get to benefit from doing that on the business side as well as directly on their bonuses,' says Kris.

Most of the strategic teams are cross-functional and across the company. Their work usually bears little relation to the day-to-day responsibilities of those involved. 'People see it as an opportunity to go beyond their normal responsibilities, and it gives them understanding of and visibility to other parts of the business. It works both ways. They get visibility and to understand other parts of the business. It is part of our leadership development process. We expect all the tier one leaders to do something cross-functional or corporate work.'

It is interesting to note that such planning processes are alive and well in such a thoroughly contemporary organisation as Infosys. The disciplined side of Infosys is combined with Google-like activities which build a culture of inclusiveness and passion for what the company is trying to achieve. On Saturdays and Sundays employees can bring their families to the campus. They come to walk around, take photographs and have picnics – though all of the Infosys cafeterias are operational during weekends. Once a year Infosys has what it calls Petite Infosys Day. Families come and there are various games and competitions, prizes and an entertainment programme. The investment in employees is significant. Just on education and training alone Infosys spends about US$100 million a year. The downturn has not affected this investment in the future.

The result is what Kris Gopalakrishnan describes as an 'open and inclusive work culture. People feel that they can give ideas and that they will be listened to, and that their ideas will be acted upon if they are good ones. There is a lot of participation in innovation and coming up with new ideas and initiatives. We encourage our employees to volunteer time for good causes. There is commitment and passion. They feel that the company has a purpose. In fact our tag line is, *Powered by intellect and values*. I think we have created a global, world-class organisation.'

There is no hubris in Kris Gopalakrishnan's statement. His belief is that if you are to compete on the world stage you must create a world-class organisation. Mediocrity is not an option.

The organism

Over 12 years, ICICI Bank has gone from an organisation of around 1000 people to a group now employing close to 100,000 people directly. Along the way structures have had to undergo continuous change as new companies came into the fold and the way it did business was reassessed, and new products came onto the market. 'To me this has also been a challenge', says K.V. Kamath. 'And it is an even bigger challenge to an organisation during turbulence or headwinds if you have a rigid organisational structure. An organisation's structure has to be like a living organism, able to change shape and character. In headwinds organisations need to look at their structure as much as the businesses.'

Kamath describes the most important elements of structure as 'the ability to basically mould itself to opportunities and to disband as those opportunities change. For example, as a business matures, you need to take out managerial layers otherwise you will very quickly have silos which become unmanageable. During the headwinds, one of the things we are going to look at is every area of cost, and this goes back to when we felt the headwinds start to build. Then we have started looking at the structure. Even if you are lean you will find areas to delayer and redo and so on. If you don't have a culture ready to accept this sort of a change, then you will have rigidity.'

Best foot forward

Agility is not only a question of organisation, it is also a state of mind. The leader in turbulent times has to be constantly alert to new opportunities – however small and fleeting they might be.

Keeping up to date with fashion trends, Sir Stuart Rose, CEO of the UK retailer Marks & Spencer (M&S) was leafing through *Vogue* when some shoes caught his eye. Next day, he went into the footwear department and asked why M&S didn't have similar style shoes in their range. On the next afternoon, the head of operations for footwear let Rose know that the shoes had now been designed and the factory in China was ready to begin production. The shoes arrived ten days later. 'I used him a lot as an example at the time', says Rose. 'It was about showing people this is a problem we can solve. A couple of youngsters were suddenly starting to say, 'Stuart, by the way I've done this.' It was sort of exponential. One guy did something I made an example of, then another guy wants to see if he can do that, then a couple more. Steve Rowe in homewear is a very aggressive trader and he began slashing the prices. We used to sell a towel rail for £21 or £22; the same towel rails of the same quality are now £9.50. That's in the space of 24 months and we're selling tens of thousands.' In any leadership role, your duty is to plant the seeds of tomorrow's value.

Fast first

When the music starts you better begin to dance. The leaders we talked to sometimes found it hard to foresee turbulent times, but all reacted quickly. Mitsubishi Corporation, for example, created a financial crisis management task force in October 2008 which involved the company's corporate management having a weekly meeting to share important information. The meetings are run by President and CEO Yorihiko Kojima.

One of these was Anand G. Mahindra, vice chairman and managing director of Mahindra & Mahindra. Founded by Anand's great-uncle and grandfather and now with revenues of US$6.7 billion, Mahindra & Mahindra is among the top 10 industrial companies in India. It is involved in automotive, farm equipment, financial services, trade and logistics, IT and infrastructure.

Anand Mahindra took a slightly circuitous route to the family business. He studied architecture in Mumbai and then film and photography at Harvard. He first joined the Mahindra Group in 1981, became the managing director in April 1997 and vice chairman in 2003. Under Anand the company launched India's best loved SUV, the Scorpio, which today has gone global.

As the headwinds hit in late 2008, Anand Mahindra moved quickly. At the company's annual conference – the Blue Chip Conference involving 500 of the company's most senior global leaders – Anand proclaimed his powerful take on the crisis. When we talked, he remembered his words:

'What does it mean for our company? I asked. We all try and use catchy acronyms or create mnemonics, but I said, there are three things we need to do.

'The first is to reboot. Essentially, a crisis means you have to go back to factory settings and re-boot. We had to go back, re-examine all our cost bases, find where we had built up fat, go back to all the low-cost platforms we had, and so on. That's hygiene.

'And the second thing we needed to do was to reinvent, to use innovation as a very strategic lever during this phase of the downturn. India's real advantage is not lowest cost to output, but lowest cost for a unit of innovation. We have to try and make sure that we are excelling at this low capital cost kind of innovation.

'The final thing I said we needed to do was to re-ignite. This is not a time to simply shut the door and wait until the storm blows over. We have to keep strategic aspirations very much in mind. We ought to be window shopping so that if the right opportunity presents itself then we will be ready to move very swiftly to consolidate our position or increase our market share. Those are the three simple things: re-boot, re-invent and re-ignite.'

This sort of sloganising is very powerful. It is a rallying cry, a shared language for the new agenda which will help create the company's future.

Taking control

Are you a rabbit caught in the headlights or in charge of your own destiny? There is no choice. Re-boot, re-invent and re-ignite would serve as a common trinity among many of the leaders we talked with.

Says Ed Dolman of Christie's: 'I do feel very much we're in charge of our own destiny, as an individual and as an organisation. We're managing for the worst and hoping for the best. We are hunkering down and working extremely hard to retain our profitability. Are we alone going to be able to restart interest in the art market and inject confidence back into that market? No. We are trying, but obviously we need lots of other things in the world economy to fall into place. But in terms of being able to adapt our business to the current climate, I do feel very much as though we're holding all the cards in our hand and we've got to play them as we see fit, and I don't feel hamstrung at all. I think it would be odd for a CEO to say that he didn't have control of his own company.'

Again we are back in crisis equals opportunity territory, but really what we're talking about is a willingness to take control, to seize the moment. As Ed Dolman put it: 'I don't think our agenda's changed. I think we may have paused, and I think that when we're able to resume and we get back into growth mode, I think we'll be in a much, much stronger position to deliver than we perhaps may have been a year or so ago, because this crisis will wipe out a hell of a lot of businesses and competitors locally and in small markets around the world that were competing against us.'

Willingness to learn

'I still believe I have a lot of areas for improvement', says Alexey Mordashov, the young CEO of Severstal. At the heart of agility is a willingness to develop and learn – individually and organisationally.

As Stephen Miles, a partner in Leadership Consulting at Heidrick & Struggles, told us, 'It's what you learn after you know everything that counts.' Other leaders we talked to were also keen to emphasise their own commitment to learning. 'Almost everybody I've worked for did a few things exceptionally well that I felt I could learn from and I've tried to have the approach that if I picked up their best characteristics it would make me a better manager and leader', said Caterpillar CEO Jim Owens. Equally frank was McDonald's CEO Jim Skinner: 'You're only as good as your last P&L, or your last performance. That's why continuous improvement is so important to me.'

Jim Skinner and Jim Owens are highly experienced global business leaders, at home in their top jobs, yet they are impressively restless to do more and to learn more. In our experience, most leaders fail because they *think* they know everything.

One and all

This restless sense of always going onto the next objective and constantly acquiring new insights and knowledge is infectious. What links the agile leaders and organisations we have encountered is that they are able to bridge the gap between individual and organisational performance. They are teams in the true sense of the word.

This has its origins in the makeup of the organisation. There is no denying the simple truth that the more diverse your team, the more creative it will be. Diversity has become business shorthand for the inclusion of women, ethnic minorities and people with disabilities. We run empowerment projects for these groups within Heidrick & Struggles but we also believe diversity should be reframed more broadly to factor in varied international and functional experience and age. True diversity should reflect the growing realities of globalisation, in all of its complexity. It should be the driving force of organisational performance. Diversity is at the heart of agile organisations.

This should hardly be controversial, but it is and progress is slow. Company boards acknowledge the need for varied international experience but improvements have often been negligible. In a survey of the UK's Most Admired Companies in 1996, 33.8 per cent of directors had international experience. By 2007 the number had only risen to 40.4 per cent.[1] There are two female CEOs in the Fortune 100 and three female CEOs in the FTSE 100;

1 Dr. Elisabeth Marx, Research into the UK's *Most Admired Companies*, Heidrick & Struggles, December 2008.

39 per cent of European companies still have no women on their boards.[2] The number of women in the boardroom has increased to 15 per cent, from 8.4 per cent from a few years ago.[3] In 2003, Norway passed a law that requires companies to have boards where women make up 40 per cent of members. In the European context, if we remove Norway, Sweden leads the way on female membership with 21.3 per cent, while Portugal comes in last with less than 1 per cent.[4]

Asia has seen a rise in the number of women in leadership and in business, especially in Singapore, Malaysia, Hong Kong and China. Our data shows the proportion of women placements at 27 per cent in China, 30 per cent in Singapore, 33 per cent in Taiwan and an average of 19.6 per cent for all of APAC (Asia Pacific). If Australia (15 per cent), New Zealand (3 per cent) and India (10 per cent) are removed from that equation, the average increases to 23 per cent.

What all this means is that too often talent is being defined in a very narrow way. If we are to stand up to the challenges of the future, and the need for organisations to strike an agile balance between people, profit and planet we need to rely on a whole range of talent – young, old, from all over the world, with different skills and experiences. The trick is in knowing how to identify it, and then unlock it.

2 Dr. Elisabeth Marx, *Route to the Top – a Transatlantic Comparison of Top Business Leaders*, Heidrick & Struggles, March 2008.
3 *Boards in Turbulent Times: Corporate Governance Report 2009: Europe*, Heidrick & Struggles, April 2009.
4 Ibid.

Progress is being made:

Releasing retirees: In the US alone there will be an estimated 56,000 senior executives reaching age of 'retirement' every year for the next 10 years. Boomers are more likely to decelerate their work than fully retire. Reasons include financial, healthcare, rising costs, and desire for intellectual engagement.

Acknowledging this trend, Heidrick & Struggles has established the Chief Advisor Network, a service to help our clients access experienced and knowledgeable talent to increase productivity, and enhance the performance of current leadership teams. Heidrick & Struggles' CAN consultants work with qualified executives who no longer wish to work 24/7. Scenarios include project management, project consulting, interim or flex-time positions, advisory board, and business coaching.

Unlocking the Facebook generation: Heidrick & Struggles is a member of think tank nGenera. An organisation established by Don Tapscott (author of, among others, *Wikinomics* and *Growing up Digital*) to investigate the needs, ambitions and attitudes of Generation Y.

nGenera's latest research project examines how young employees can be properly engaged in the workplace to help drive revenue.

The female side: We believe the argument for more women in the boardroom and on top executive teams needs to be reframed as an economic, not a gender-based consideration. New fund Naissance Capital is studying 170 companies, to explore how female leadership affects the performance of companies. The initial results tell us that companies that have more women at the top are outperforming companies that do not. Based on this research, Naissance will create a fund that invests only in companies where gender diversity is a driver of business.

Sceptics might suggest that all of this is a hill of righteous beans. Not so. At the heart of the corporation of the future will be a commitment to balance in all aspects of an organisation's activities. From balance springs agility.

Resources

W. Chan Kim and Renée Mauborgne, *Blue Ocean Strategy*, Harvard Press, 2006

Nirmalya Kumar et al., *India's Global Powerhouses*, Harvard Press, 2009

Tom Peters and Robert Waterman, *In Search of Excellence*, Harper, 1982

Don Tapscott, *Growing Up Digital: Rise of the Net Generation*, McGraw-Hill Inc, 1999

Don Tapscott and Anthony D. Williams, *Wikinomics: How Mass Collaboration Changes Everything*, Portfolio, 2006

7 Living with turbulence

> *'Keeping your energy going is at different levels. First, you have to discover something exciting to do in the organisational context. You have to try and celebrate the building of the vision. You have to work with younger people to keep your energies going. You have to have an entrepreneurial mindset, and I think finally you also need to reinvent yourself every year. In today's world you are obsolete if you are not doing that. If I look at the last 10 years, if I hadn't reinvented myself I would have fallen by the wayside long ago.'*
>
> K.V. Kamath, ICICI Bank

Giving it all

There's a powerful children's book called *The Giving Tree* by Shel Silverstein. It is a story about a tree and a little boy.

Every day the boy comes to swing on the tree's branches, to eat its apples and sleep in its shade. The boy loves the tree. And the tree loves the boy. But as the years pass the boy finds other things to do and the tree is often alone.

After much time has passed, the boy comes to the tree and asks for money. The tree suggests he picks its apples and sells them in the city. This makes the boy happy; he picks all the apples and goes away. And he stays away for a long time.

One day the boy comes back – he wants to build himself a house. The tree suggests he cuts off its branches. This makes the boy happy; he cuts off all of the tree's branches and goes away to build his house.

He stays away for a long time and is old when he returns. He is unhappy and fed up with life and wants a boat so that he can sail far away. The tree tells him to saw its trunk in two and make a boat. This makes the boy happy; he hollows the tree's trunk into a boat and sails away.

The tree (now a tree stump) is alone. After many years, the boy comes back; he is now very old and sad. And the tree is sad too, because he feels he has nothing left to give the boy.

The boy tells the tree that he is just so very tired and needs to sit down. The tree suggests that the boy sits on his stump and rests. And the boy does, and the tree is happy; it was wrong when it thought it had no more to give the boy.

Being a leader can feel like being a giving tree. At work, and at home, people need you to give more. And as the turbulence mounts, the calls on the leader's time increase exponentially. We demand a lot from our top people. More now than perhaps at any other point in the last century. Forget about 9 to 5, or 7 to 7, or 6 till 10. The cell phone, Internet and BlackBerry changed all that. Now we can work 24 hours a day, across every region in the world. Ever spent an afternoon at the in-laws' quietly closing a deal? Ever gone on vacation and thought, just a little peek at my email won't hurt? Leading in turbulent times demands huge reservoirs of energy, will, and stamina. But how can leaders manage this? How can they survive?

Among our interviewees five sanity-preserving factors emerged. They fall into our three categories of Passion, People skills and Maintaining a Big Picture Vision.

Passion:

1. the ability to accentuate the positive whenever possible;
2. a willingness to see opportunities for self-development.

People skills:

3. to show kindness and sincerity towards yourself and others;
4. the ability to look after yourself physically and mentally, but also a willingness to accept support when it is offered.

Vision:

5. maintaining a sense of context.

It's not life or death ... usually

'I've been through six of these', said PwC's Sam DiPiazza. 'I joined the firm in '73 and that was the last time we had as big a drop in demand and it was the oil crisis that caused it. It was nasty, but I didn't realise it was happening because I was a brand new staff guy. Today, most of our young partners, 42 or 43 years old, were also relatively new staff people during the last big recession in 1991. So this is the first time they've seen it, and that's why you have to keep a measured response.'

It was surprising how calm and aware of the historical context the leaders we talked to were. Lawson's Takeshi Niinami provided an interesting take on leading during crisis. He conceded that he was busier than ever before, often clocking up 120 hour weeks. He viewed turbulence as an opportunity to really accelerate human development in the organisation. Much of his time is spent supporting and guiding his management team as they weather their first crisis. 'I've found more talented people than before', he told us with enthusiasm. 'People working together is the key if you are to overcome this kind of crisis. I have changed the management team totally over five years, but I want young managers to go through it themselves. The new guys will pick up a lot of experience and absorb it.'

A real crisis brings out the philosopher in the world's leaders. For some, a global crisis is actually and somewhat strangely a relief. Suddenly, the playing field is levelled. We are all in trouble. 'From a stress standpoint, even though you've got your own, at least you know you are not the only person who is dealing with the magnitude of challenge that's out there. And I think there has to be a bit of comfort in that', reflects Linda Wolf of Leo Burnett.

'Part of what helps me is a sense of context, I think, knowing that this is a stressful situation, the market's going to hell and the economy is tough, etc., and as a result of that we need to do some creative and appropriate and nimble things to get back. But those are all opportunities, those are not people dying', says Kaiser Permanente's George Halvorson.

Retaining a sense of perspective lies at the heart of the business philosophy of Severstal's Alexey Mordashov. 'It's important to look at the fundamentals, not for the business, but for you. I ask myself, "Is it your choice?" "Would you like to continue?" And sometimes it's difficult and tough, but it's my life. I've chosen it consciously, deliberately, and voluntarily, and I'm thinking, basically, get on with it. Of course, you see tough times, and good times. You have to be prepared. This should be an important feature in the culture and the mindset of all executives in mature industries, because all mature industries are cyclical.'

The glass is half full ... always

'It's very difficult to keep a positive attitiude constantly. It's difficult to be upbeat at meetings, but people look at you to do that', admits Bijan Khosrowshahi, who was CEO of Fuji Fire and Marine. Bijan is exactly right and this was a point reinforced by all the leaders we talked to. The leader sets the tone and a positive tone trumps negativity every time – no matter what the situation. 'A leader is a dealer in hope', Napoleon once observed.

'It's your job to have a cup half full, it's your role to provide that enthusiasm and positive energy to the organisation', says Mark Frissora of Hertz. 'But how do you do it?', we countered.

'I think you've got to be predisposed that way. Winners always typically view the world that way. Having that cup-half-full attitude helps you get through life, makes you more successful, and it's what I preach to my management team. You guys walk out of a room and you've got a frown on your face, everyone in the organisation will be depressed, and you'll take your organisation right down the proverbial toilet. The shadow of a leader is huge so it's very important that we walk out of this room with smiles on our faces, and talk about the opportunities. We need discipline, but at the same time we need to make sure that we always put a positive frame of reference on everything we're doing. I've always been built that way, so I'm always looking for where's the next way to make more money, get more revenue, drive more costs, or efficiency.'

Richard Langan, the CEO of North American law firm Nixon Peabody, capped his 20+ years legal career at the firm by being elected its CEO at the start of 2008. This thrust him into the senior leadership role at the most turbulent of times. For Dick, balancing how he communicates the passion he feels for his firm and its future, with the need to respond quickly to extremely challenging demands caused by the global downturn in demand for legal service has become the cornerstone of his leadership. 'Difficult economic times require leaders to establish a good balance between optimism and realism. Since the great recession set in, I've worked relentlessly to convey my strong belief in the firm's vision and future success together with highlighting the need for heightened vigilance. With passion, a leader can motivate others to give 110 per cent and maintain infectious enthusiasm in the face of concerns over the economic uncertainties.'

Leaders are, somewhat fortunately perhaps, born optimists. They believe in the future – no matter how dreadful the present. Ed Dolman of Christie's is definitely in the glass half full category. 'You know, it could be worse. That's what I keep saying to myself. It could be worse, and I'm grateful that we can adapt quite quickly. I am grateful that we're in the business we are in, even though we're all so highly affected by the destruction of personal wealth that's happened worldwide', he told us. 'Luckily we're not a public company. We were public until 1998, and then we were bought by a private individual, François Pinault, and I thank my lucky stars every day that I don't have to make public pronouncements on performance.'

Blind optimism is not what is required, emphasises Tom Glocer: 'You have got to get the balance right. Your investors don't want somebody who doesn't have a clue as to how serious it is. You have got to be honest with your employees.'

Among the people we talked to one of the most philosophically optimistic was Alexey Mordashov, CEO of Severstal, Russia's largest steelmaker and said to be one of Russia's best-run businesses. Severstal hired Mordashov, in his early twenties, as an economist in 1988. He went on to secure outright control of the firm and became chief executive in 1996. Hit hard by the financial downturn, Mordashov was calm and collected when we spoke.

'I don't see any significant changes in my view on the world, long term. The world remains a competitive place. What is happening, is just the normal consequence of the free market. Fundamentally what is happening is understandable and generally good. The best proven way to improve quality of life is the free market economy', he said.

Personal development

As well as a keen sense of the historical and economic context of turbulence and positivity at all times, leaders retain a constant commitment to improving themselves and their organisations. They recognise that no one is perfect. Leaders also need to develop and improve. This is surprisingly difficult. It is a bit like trying to get fit when you are in the middle of a title fight.

It begins with questions, asking questions of yourself. 'Now more than any other time, you have to make the separation so work doesn't influence your personal life and family. I like exercise, for example, and try very hard not to let all the things that are happening eat into that. It's critical', says Bijan Khosrowshahi, formerly of Fuji. 'As a leader you need to sit down and think about the decisions you have made, take responsibility for them and come to terms with them. To keep your head straight, you have to focus on going forward. You have to focus on saying that's okay, this has happened. How do we go forward and how do we get the company to move forward to the next level?'

In a world where knowledge is a critical organisational asset, great emphasis is placed on personal development.

Corporate universities, e-learning programmes, in-house training, personal learning networks, these are just a few of the learning options available to employees. But what is available for those higher up the organisation? What about a chief marketing officer (CMO) who wants to hone their leadership skills, acquire a deeper self-knowledge or maybe just retain their edge both mentally and physically?

The higher up you are the harder it is to do personal development. For a start, who delivers it? When you get to the top of the organisation the issues you are dealing with are much more around leadership style, personal effectiveness, and interpersonal skills such as empathy, communication, listening, impact, clarity, and this is feedback and coaching that is very hard to give to anyone who is more senior than you or who is a colleague.

Externally, executive education programmes and leadership forums are options. But many senior executives are too busy running teams and organisations to take the time out to attend.

Just a few years ago, news that a senior executive was using a coach would have raised eyebrows in the boardroom. Today, however, assigning an executive coach to improve a leader's management performance and/or overcome their personal development deficiencies is a far more acceptable practice.

For senior executives, the attractions of employing a coach are obvious. There is no need to leave the office for a start – a major plus for time-strapped executives. Better still, the coach fits into the executive's timetable, and provides a tailor-made programme focused solely on the needs of the executive.

Then there is the important issue of trust and confidentiality. 'We have this idea of organisations as pyramids, so at the top there's only space for one person. Also there are tactical reasons in the following sense: careers are individualistic, people are just not prepared for or used to sharing power. People are not used to trusting someone', reflects Professor José-Luis Álvarez. Sad but true, yet trust underpins the coaching relationship. 'An executive coach provides a safe place. Who else can leaders turn to? They are surrounded by senior managers who drink from the same water fountain', says one coach. Today, coaches who work with the most senior levels of leaders see themselves, and are viewed by their clients, as trusted advisers with a unique perspective on the leader and organisation with which they are working.

Looking after yourself

'I try to keep positive, even with the headlights on me, so I really think that having a positive attitude and a sincere love for the job you do keeps energy levels high. I try to have some time for myself also, I exercise every day, I eat well, make time to share with my family and friends. And, well and obviously I drink at least one Modelo a day', replied Carlos Fernandez when we asked him about how he looked after himself in turbulent times. Equally, he was adamant that part of his job was to broaden the sense of responsibility in the company. 'I try to make clear that it's not only me that works in the company, so I need the help of everyone. I need the help of the team to be positive, and one of the things that I also like to tell them is that I feel proud of working with them, because they are talented, a great team and we have gone through many things that are very difficult to handle, so I really feel proud of them and they should be proud of working for this company.'

Looking to develop skills and new perspectives has to be combined with physical and mental fortitude.

'I tend to ratchet up physical activity in times of stress, so a bit more in the gym, a bit more tennis', Tom Glocer, CEO of Thomson Reuters, told us. ' I've got young kids. I think the first thing in life is you've got to have is a really stable home platform. Which isn't to say that even in the happiest and most normal home there aren't stresses.'

Anand Mahindra was one of the many leaders who talked to us about how they looked after themselves. Anand has a long-established workout routine to ensure he is physically up to the job. And then, as he explains, adrenaline kicks in: 'When you do a big deal the adrenaline is something that you don't anticipate and it's a huge booster. We've seen that with a lot of people when they get into a position of much greater responsibility, influence and accountability, the adrenalin comes naturally. And I think you need that whole elusive work–life balance. This is not the time to forget about it. That's where I think I have a secret weapon and that's my wife who functions as my coach and guru. She certainly keeps me honest and makes me remember that there's a family, that there's another world. That balance, I think, is going to be absolutely critical. If you don't maintain a balance and you get obsessive about any one thing, I think the only decisions you'll make will be the wrong ones.'

Balancing acts

Work–life balance was a constant refrain – even in turbulent times.

'I think balance is essential; you don't do as good a job if you don't have some of that balance; and you get it wherever you can. It's basic stuff like exercise and also finding those moments when you can gain additional insight in whatever other area you might feel is appropriate. You can work yourself to death but in the end you're not going to add as much value', says Linda Wolf.

Working more hours is not the answer, advised PwC's Sam DiPiazza. 'You're not going to solve this problem by working 20 hours a day. You have to be smarter, and that means you have to stay fresh and alert. You have to keep a level of balance, otherwise the big judgements you make right now, which are really tough judgements, you're not going to make at the top of your game', he said.

When we spoke Sam had just been to India to deal with a problem. He made sure that the day before he left he did nothing but relax – 'I didn't do anything and my wife and I took a nice long walk in Zurich. I think every executive has to keep that balance in their life or they'll find themselves making a lot of bad decisions.'

Definitely in the balanced category is Chip McClure of ArvinMeritor. We asked him about his schedule. 'I tend to get in early. I think the only person that gets in before me in the morning is my CFO [chief financial officer]. I'm usually in by 6.30; he's in by 6.00 so he's got the coffee made, which is nice', he told us. 'There is no average week. If I look at my calendar for a full year, there's obviously certain things which are locked in – starting with board meetings, committee meetings, various shareholder meetings, analyst meetings, earnings calls, that type of thing. So within each week there may be those kind of things interspersed.

'If I look at next week, on Monday I'm meeting with one of our heavy truck customers; on Tuesday and Wednesday I'm going to be in Washington, DC. One of the things I try to do is spend time in Washington not only as a representative of the company, but also to represent the automotive industry. So I've got a number of Capitol Hill visits with senators, and congresspeople. Then on Thursday I'm visiting with a company that's totally outside of our industry, just to do some benchmarking on technology. The company I'm meeting with has done a tremendous job reinventing itself by developing innovative technology. Then the following week I'll be visiting some of our global facilities. Two weeks ago I was in Mexico and visited six or seven of our plants. Obviously, I spent the majority of my time with our people, but at a few of the facilities I also took the time to meet with some of the local elected officials.'

Chip is famed for his ability to ensure that meetings run on time. 'The only thing you can't recapture is time', he says. He has three strategically placed clocks in his office. 'These clocks are in place because I don't normally like meetings to last more than an hour. I understand that sometimes a meeting might have to go a little longer because of the content, but when we hit 45 minutes and haven't gotten through all of the items, I'll say, "Listen, we've got 15 minutes left, what do we need to get resolved? Let's get it resolved, and let's move on. Because there's only 24 hours in a day."'

The roads travelled

Energy is undoubtedly a prerequisite for leading in turbulent times. Leaders also expect it of the people they work with. Energy levels are most obviously tested by the vast amounts of travel which come as part of the job. 'I travel a great deal', one chief operating officer (COO) told us. 'My home office is in a suburb of Washington, DC, but I spent a great deal of my time on the road – in excess of 50 per cent. So I am in the office less than half the time.'

That's pretty typical. The reality as a twenty-first century leader is that you are on the road most of the week. You do overnight flights because you're commuting, and when you get to the weekend you're tired, and perhaps not as patient as you should be. Says Caterpillar's Jim Owens: 'I don't know how you can be a CEO and not know how to sleep on an airplane. I sleep about as well overnight to Europe as I do at home in bed.'

The reality is that extensive travelling is a prerequisite for anyone in a top job if they are to help their organisation maintain its competitive edge. Business relationships are based on communication and, as we've seen, communication is the cornerstone of any top job. The question is why all the new communication media have failed to make a dent in travel schedules? The answer seems to lie with a simple statistic. More than 80 per cent of human communication is non-verbal (some studies put it as high as 93 per cent). In other words, email, telephone, video conferencing, and all the other communications marvels do not have the bandwidth to carry more than 20 per cent of the face-to-face experience.

Facial expressions, body language, eye contact – these are key conduits. Without them you can't get past first base. It's tough to bond over the Internet. So, unless your client is in the next office, to do business you have to travel. How else can you meet customers, colleagues and competitors? 'A CEO from Switzerland told me once that he has a personal key performance indicator that he wants to meet twice as many customers as investors and I think that's a very good target', says Monika Ribar of Panalpina.

At Caterpillar, Jim Owens travels the world attending employee meetings. With over 300 significant facilities scattered across 40 countries, it is impossible for Owens to visit every one every year, but he tries to ensure that an executive officer from HQ in Peoria gets to every major facility. 'That's a lot of getting out', he reflects, 'but I like to be sure that at least one of us appears there and has a chance to have a dialogue and talk to people, make them feel like they're a critical part of our organisation everywhere we do business.'

The downsides of constant travel are well documented, and justifiably so. Less emphasised are the plus sides. As a well-travelled leader you get to meet a huge number of people and develop relationships which are important to them as businesspeople and as human beings. Travel allows people to connect. It can be a richly rewarding personal experience. Travel not only broadens the expense account. Business trips offer new and exciting vistas.

Making space

Ask leaders how they factor in some downtime and you will get a bunch of different answers. One they will all tell you, though, is even if, and especially if, you are a global CEO, you still need to take some time out to unwind, both physically and mentally.

One CFO told us about visiting another corporation where busyness reigned supreme. 'Every day there were two or three firm-wide new initiatives. Everybody had open calendars. The entire day, nine hours a day, was controlled by somebody else. People had to go to meetings but they didn't know what they were about. People were bombarded with ideas that weren't screened. If you wanted to manage your career up, you had to invest three or four hours a day just catching up with the news in the company. You can't manage a company like that. You overload.'

Loyal supporters

With huge demands on their limited time and a punishing travel schedule, the leader – any leader – needs support.

There is a central paradox to being a leader: it is the most prominent and eye-catching role, but it can also be the loneliest. As a leader you get the attention, you get the welcome at the airport, the welcoming committee when you visit an office. Then you are sitting in a taxi on the way back to the airport and you know it is your name which will go against the decision.

Leaders realise pretty soon that they need support from every network they can lay their hands on. As a leader it doesn't take long to see that it is a very different job from any other position. Days are longer and busier than ever. They travel constantly. The impression the leader gives tells people how the company is doing; they need to be up, positive and engaged, all the time.

During the research for this book, the incredible patience of the leaders' spouses has come up again and again. Leaders nearly always mention their home life and the insight and support they couldn't do without.

'Running a mega-company, like Caterpillar, is about having a great leadership team, great cohesion, understanding of the business and industry, so you can lay out the broad strategic direction, stake out very bold goals for what you hope to achieve, and then working with a great team of people, who really understand all aspects of the business and can cascade that down to a work agenda for the whole organisation', says Caterpillar's Jim Owens. 'Also, it'd be very difficult to have this job and not have a wife who was a partner. My wife is just great support. We've moved the family around the world – Geneva, Switzerland, Djakarta, Indonesia, Nassau, San Diego, back and forth to Peoria. She does that with full recognition of everything I've got to do and the fact that she's got to do a lot of things with me, if we're going to stay together as a team.'

The domestic anchor and support mechanism was universal. 'Any time with my family, daughter and friends restores me', says Kris Gopalakrishnan of Infosys. 'The good thing is the family also has a lot of ownership of Infosys. It is a company they have seen from the beginning and have benefited from. The family support is important. Time we spend with friends and family is important. I get energised by interacting with people who are as passionate as I am, people who also feel that there are many more things to be done and that there are a lot of issues. If I can contribute in some way I feel energised.'

Support begins at home, but turbulence and the extra demands it brings inevitably take a toll on home life. Leaders tend to inhabit two separate worlds, with everyone demanding their time and attention. Talking with Richard Baker, when he was CEO of Alliance Boots, he told of how he broke his shoulder when he fell out of a tree because he was just trying to be a good dad. His daughter wanted to climb a tree but he was tired from jet lag and working away all week, so he wasn't really concentrating as he climbed. He missed his step and fell to the ground. Tired leaders and trees don't mix!

All the leaders we talked to, and have talked to over the years, reveal much the same trouble with balancing hectic schedules and family life. The family is the ultimate support network. 'I take my family vacations, I spend time with my kids and wife and carve it out. But, you know, you've got to work about as hard at that as you do your job', says Jim Owens, CEO of Caterpillar.

It was an issue also tackled by Jim Skinner of McDonald's. 'You know, we all work hard. I've seen a lot of people work hard and they confuse effort with results, and that's a danger. I think that's sort of dumbing down the whole concept around hard work. I'd rather say, let's work smart. It makes more sense.'

Says Peter Sharpe, CEO of Cadillac Fairview: 'I've always worked a lot and long hours, but I rarely ever bring work home. I've always been able to, to close the door of the office and make that break. I love what I do and I enjoy time with my family, but you sacrifice a lot if you aspire to grow and run an organisation. There's lots of sacrifices along the way.'

Close at hand

At work there are a variety of support mechanisms. Many companies now have a COO who manages internally, while the CEO devotes more attention to what's going on outside. It is not a new idea. There are precedents. Examples of famous business double acts abound. Think of David Hewlett and Bill Packard, James Hanson and Gordon White, Microsoft founders Bill Gates and Paul Allen, Body Shop's Gordon and Anita Roddick. Richard Branson relies on his sidekick of many years, Will Whitehorn. More recently, David Filo and Jerry Yang, the founders of Yahoo!, styled themselves chief Yahoos.

Stephen Miles, a partner in Leadership Consulting at Heidrick & Struggles, has done a lot of work on the role of the COO. He sounds a note of caution about the COO/CEO relationship in his book (co-authored with Nathan Bennett) *Riding Shotgun*. He notes: 'The key ingredient for COO effectiveness is often whether the CEO is ready to share power. Unfortunately some COOs do not realise the CEO is not ready until they are in the position and friction begins to appear in the relationship.'[1]

But most leaders today, at least in theory, seem to understand that solo leadership in the corporate world is ultimately inefficient and ineffective. No one individual, no matter how gifted, can be right all the time; no one individual, particularly in a large organisation, has the relevant information to make every important decision. Over time, resources become misallocated, opportunities are missed, innovation becomes stifled. Over-control saps initiative and bureaucratic behaviour ensues.

Whether you like it or not, a leader has to rely on others – their secretary; their spouse; their colleagues; their team; their friends; their BlackBerry and many more. If you fly solo you go round in circles.

The perfect chair

At the very top, the relationship between the CEO and the chairman is key. 'I have a very close exchange with my chairman', says Monika Ribar of Panalpina. 'I try to talk to him, certainly at least once a week or even twice a week, to inform him, to talk to him, to also get his feedback.'

With boards becoming more independent and the chairman's role being split from the CEO, the CEO–chairman–board of directors relationship will be increasingly crucial to how a company performs.

1 Nathan Bennett and Stephen A. Miles, *Riding Shotgun: The Role of the COO*, Stanford Business Books, 2006, p. 5.

Historically, the CEO and chairman roles were often combined in American corporations. Separation is now commonplace thanks to corporate governance guidelines requiring greater distance between the board and the CEO to encourage objectivity.

A study by the governance ratings firm GovernanceMetrics International (GMI) found that 95 per cent of the FTSE 350 firms rated by GMI split the roles of CEO and chairman. In France, where the combined CEO and chairman has traditionally been a powerful force, there is now movement in this direction, with companies such as Renault and Carrefour splitting the roles. In Germany, the roles of the chairman as head of the supervisory board and of the CEO as head of the management board are separated in law.

More companies are splitting the chairman and CEO positions between two people. A survey by Institutional Shareholder Services of 1433 companies that make up the various Standard & Poor's indexes, including the S&P 500, found that 41 per cent had separate chairmen and CEO positions in 2006, up from 37 per cent in 2005.

It is also notable that some high-profile CEOs have become chairmen of major corporations. This suggests that they see the roles as powerful rather than ambassadorial – examples include former Nokia CEO Jorma Ollia becoming chairman of Shell; and AstraZeneca recruiting Louis Schweitzer, the ex-Renault boss, as its chairman.

When it comes to healthy CEO–chairman relationships,

best practice is rarely reported. Agreement between CEO and chairman is not a great media story. There is a wide range of approaches. Some chairmen are hands-on whereas others have a light touch. There is no formula. Successful instances often involve founders moving from the CEO's job to become chairman. Consider Microsoft chairman and CEO Bill Gates handing over the CEO reins to long-time colleague Steve Ballmer in 2000; eBay company founder Pierre Omidyar becoming non-executive chairman with Meg Whitman as CEO; and Intel's Andy Grove becoming chairman with Craig Barrett as CEO.

In reality, the most effective boards are high-performance teams. As with all effective teams, members have clearly defined roles, play to their strengths and complement each other. CEOs need to think of boards as part of their team rather than as a sometimes irritating supervisory body.

The board is seen by the leaders we talked to as a vital network. 'I've heard it said that the board provides the cheapest advice the CEO will ever get. I've been a consultant for a large part of my career and, as a board member, the company and CEO have free access to me', says Heidrick & Struggles board member Jill Kanin-Lovers. 'That's why I think who you put on your board also is very important. It is not uncommon when someone becomes the new CEO, and they take a look at the board, for them to say, "Hey, I could use maybe some counsel in this area and I don't see it reflected on this board", or, "You know, maybe there are folks on this board who I don't think are giving me fresh thinking."

Not only do we provide oversight, but we're in essence a tool, a resource to the CEO, and they want to make sure they've got the right composition to reflect that.'

Feeling good, doing good, having fun

There is a final element to all of this: the leaders we have encountered over the years have always wanted to build something, achieve something fantastic, to do something special. Their motives go far beyond simply making money. 'When I was asked if I wanted to lead Mumtalakat I knew that this was my opportunity to give something back to the country that has given me so much', said Talal Al Zain of Bahrain's Mumtalakat Holding Company.

Effective leaders are never one-dimensional. 'Whether it's skiing or travelling or reading or cooking, I've got all kinds of things that I'm interested in', said Linda Wolf when we asked her about her interests. 'Plus the not-for-profit area, I think that's a place where you can take your business discipline and use it in a different way. It fulfils you in a different way because you're giving back, you're hopefully helping, you're moving the organisation or project or whatever it is forward; but you're doing it solely based on the fact that you care about it; you're not getting any financial reward for it; you're just getting the reward of helping somebody accomplish something.'

Says Gary Knell of Sesame Workshop: 'At the end of the day, you've got to have fun at this job. When this stops becoming something that you get up in the morning and are really enthusiastic about coming in to tackle every day, it's probably time to move on.'

Importantly, having fun increases productivity. It makes people work harder, faster, smarter. The reality is that firms that focus on fun are more productive. When companies show a commitment to something bigger than the profit motive, they build loyalty and show soul. Firms that focus on making fun a part of their culture build a better work–life balance, which in turn means healthier, more motivated employees. It is the same for those in top jobs, where CSR and philanthropy can provide a sense of purpose beyond hitting earnings targets.

To some this sounds superficial, but it's not just about doing good, it also has to make sound business sense.

Resources

José Luis Álvarez and Silviya Svejenova, *Sharing Executive Power*, Cambridge University Press, 2005

Nathan Bennett and Stephen A. Miles, *Riding Shotgun: The Role of the COO*, Stanford Business Books, 2006

Marshall Goldsmith (with Mark Reiter), *What Got You Here Won't Get You There*, Hyperion, 2007

8 The leading in turbulent times checklist

'What often happens when you have a time of crisis and things get really tense and don't go quite the way you would like them to is that you all work better than ever before.'

John Brock, Coca-Cola Enterprises

As we come to the end of our navigation story we want to remind you of the three key ingredients needed for any leader in these turbulent times: passion, people skills (especially communication) and maintaining a long-term big vision.

Passion

Seizing the day

Turbulence will continue but that does not mean that opportunities come to an end. 'Don't change your dreams, that's what I would say', advises PwC's Sam DiPiazza. 'Don't rashly decide, well, with all this uncertainty, I'm not going to pursue my long-held ambitions in finance, I'm going to go be a window washer. It might take a couple of years but this will pass, so keep investing in yourself and fight your way through it. If you invest in yourself, keep your dream, you will find a bridge from here to there.'

Ask yourself, how can we benefit from this? How can we come out the other side stronger? 'I'm a very positive guy to begin with', says Victor Fung. 'I get myself fired up, and our people fired up by thinking about the opportunity side of the crisis. The initial reaction of course is fire fighting, everywhere you're putting out fires, but very soon you say, hey, look, out of all this there's a real opportunity, and start focusing on some of the opportunities. How we can strengthen ourselves. How we can strengthen our entire staff building skills? How do we improve our market position in the industry as we face this downturn? By focusing on the opportunity, I think we manage to energise ourselves.'

Becoming agile

Are you taking the initiative? Create a programme which sets a positive agenda. Faced with turbulence, Henry Fernandez created a campaign called *Follow the Money.* 'I said, look, the money has shifted quite dramatically', he explains. 'The big asset management companies have centralised and frozen budgets, there is no money to be made there but there are a lot of other clients that have budgets – midsize institutions, small ones, pension funds and the like. So, *Follow the Money*. People have been really engaged and very creative. I focus them away from the newspaper problem, as I call it, and people got re-energised because all of a sudden they felt that they could control their destiny as opposed to feeling despair and a lack of control by looking at what was going on in the world.'

People skills

Developing a global perspective

Develop your CQ (cultural quotient). The ability to lead through different cultures across the globe and communicate effectively has never been more important.

'The CQ is certainly crucial', says Victor Fung. 'It's all one world now in every sense of the word and every problem is interconnected with every other problem. So you're going to have to deal on a very broad gauge basis and need to be able to communicate across cultures. Also I think you have to be really information technology savvy and sensitive to the consequences of an interconnected world.'

Developing your antennae

Why? When? Where? Who? How? Do you routinely ask questions of others and yourself? The ability to ask yourself difficult questions is at the heart of communicating. Bijan Khosrowshahi, formerly CEO of Fuji Fire and Marine says: 'Is my communication working? Is the message that I want to send out working? But on the other side you have to have some receptors to say how was it received.' The trouble is that the further you move up the corporate hierarchy the less likely you are you have honest audience members who will give you a frank assessment on how effectively you are communicating. (As a side point here, it is interesting to note how many successful leaders have trusted sidekicks who have travelled alongside them and act as their eyes and ears in the organisation.)

How do you collect and maximise information? In turbulent times there is a premium put on information. 'In my opinion, when the economy is in recession, a significant task of management is to seek various kinds of information', says Wang Jianzhou of China Mobile. 'Now I spend more time in acquiring information. I follow financial news, stock market information, as well as information concerning ICT development. The demand changes in the telecom market are my greatest concern.'

Managing people

People always. 'I live with a motto of treasuring every encounter with people', Yorihiko Kojima, President and CEO of Mitsubishi Corporation told us. 'Our strength lies in trust from our stakeholders. It is important to strengthen trust-based relationships inside the company.'

People will always ask questions. Bring them onboard or count them out. 'If you get somebody who's really a tough bird, always positioning for more money, always pushing the envelope, you bring them in early and make them part of the solution', advises PwC's Sam DiPiazza. 'Let them know, I need your help here, you've got to help us through this. If then they continue to say, well, what about me me me, you've got to deal with them straight up, because whatever you do the whole organisation is watching. These days, you know, nobody is going to be a real winner, it's more of a question of just how big the losers will be.'

Trust breeds trust

Jill Kanin-Lovers draws from her experience as a board member, to comment: 'There has been a lot of talk about agility focused on business operations. Cultural agility is equally important. During the past 10 years I have served on the Board of Directors for five corporations, all in completely different industries. Each has had to address business challenges, some more pressing than others. I have participated in numerous acquisitions, divestitures, and, as a sign of the times, an unfortunate Chapter 11 filing.

'One of my key learnings is how effective strong leadership which emphasises trust is the driver in making the workforce agile. This can't be something that you decide to 'implement' as part of a business crisis plan – it has to be there before the crisis hits. No one wants a reduction-in-force programme, but as a board member, I have seen the difference in how a programme is accepted and implemented based on the trust that existed beforehand. Treating those exiting with respect and dignity is critical for keeping the 'survivors' engaged and agile in addressing new business issues.

'In the recent economic crisis, many companies have had to take actions never anticipated before. It has been a real test of leadership and a reflection of the trust that was cultivated previously. I was particularly impressed by two examples. First, one company for which I am a director, announced a one-day reduction in the working week for employees at a service centre. Rather than being greeted with cynicism, the employees actually gave the leadership team a standing ovation. The employees trusted management and knew they were trying to save jobs.

'At another company, the process of letting people go was done with such and care and sensitivity that the

CEO received notes from employees in the organisation saying how proud they were of how this difficult situation was handled. In earlier years, RIFs [reductions in force] had taken place in this organisation for similar business reasons, but the results were disastrous. The former CEO (before my time) had not built the degree of trust throughout the organisation that this new CEO has. The lack of trust existed independently of the business decision. After this, the organisation really struggled to get back on track as the workforce lacked the agility to move forward. Under the new CEO, the organisation was immediately galvanised to address the business realities. As a leader you need to make the tough calls – but you also need the organisation to be agile enough to not only bounce back but thrive going forward.'

Remember that your customers are people too. They also need and require your soft side skills to keep them loyal and committed to your enterprise. How many customers do you meet? Customers are the lifeblood of any business. We asked Kris Gopalakrishnan of Infosys about the most significant change to his working habits brought about the upsurge in turbulence. 'I am in front of our customers more, which I think is to be expected', he said simply.

Communicating

Is your communication honest and upfront? Really? As we have seen, people respond positively if they get the full story, unvarnished by spin, unkeepable promises or bull. One company we talked to told its employees that the annual sales jamboree in Florida was going to be cancelled. The company felt that not flying hundreds of people to Tampa was a worthwhile saving. It expected there would be uproar from dissatisfied sales execs denied their winter sun and margaritas. A webcast seemed something of a limp replacement, but the CEO explained that the choice was stark: Tampa or a large cash saving and the saving of jobs. This straight talking actually concentrated people's minds and turned their focus on making tough decisions in their workplaces.

How transparent are your communications? Be open otherwise you run the risk of your messages being hijacked.

'Your employees are part of multiple groups, multiple communities and multiple social networks. Everybody can blog and publish. There is no way you can prevent information from coming out. It can come out in multiple ways. You have to make sure that you have higher levels of transparency. With every decision that is communicated internally we have to expect that it can become headlines in the newspapers. We must be prepared and ready for that', says Kris Gopalakrishnan of Infosys.

What barriers to communication exist in your organisation? How can you remove them? Culture, corporate history and engrained behaviours stalk the corporate corridors. The leader's job must be to remove barriers to communication of all sorts. 'There are two problems with communications', says Severstal's Alexey Mordashov in a typically honest assessment of his own company. 'Some parts of the company have just not been with the company long enough to be integrated well enough. It's a challenge, and communication should help, but people often just don't know the rules. And not all parts of the company are up to date with the changes required by the free market economy. The degree of bureaucracy, red tape, in many parts of the company, is very high, and it's a great impediment to communication. And we just have to remove it.' And so say all of us.

Long-term vision

Thinking big while fighting fires

Think big at all times. 'Always try and keep the big picture in mind – where do we want to go? It can be too easy to be sucked into fire fighting in tough times,' advises Talal Al Zain. 'Yes, you need to go into detail but it's important you don't stay there. You need to regularly look around you, stay engaged with others and find out what's happening in the world outside of your organisation.'

Learning to love uncertainty while you maintain your vision

Uncertainty is a fact of commercial life. Face the facts. Says Nick Stephan of Phoenix Partners: 'You get more and more comfortable with the uncertainty. You figure out what your worst case scenario is going to be, prepare for it and try to improve from there. And that's how we've attacked this problem and we're now at a point where we're okay with this.'

Clearly stating what you value

What are the key measures of success? An organisation's culture and outlook is formed by how success is measured by its leaders. Mark Frissora of Hertz says: 'I believe in running a business on three principles, and around three things. Customer satisfaction, employee satisfaction, and cash management. And I don't let any one of those three things ever get out of balance, because I've always found that if you decide you want to cut things with employees, eventually your customer satisfaction or your cash management goes down. The same thing is true with any one of those three things, you cut one, and it has a direct relationship on the other two. Eventually the other two are compromised. So we keep all of our measurements in the company equally focused around those three areas. Keeping that balance, keeping investing in people even in tough times, celebrating successes, constantly rewarding and recognising people that are doing a good job during these adverse times: that's how you keep the positive energy in the organisation.'

Building organisational radar for future storms and opportunities

Turbulence is the new reality. How far ahead are you looking? What does the next downturn look like? Are you ready? 'The world has moved enough in the direction that Tom Friedman[1] talks about, the world is flat. Thanks to IT and logistics, the response time is being shortened more and more', says Victor Fung. 'Before it

1 Thomas L. Friedman, *The World Is Flat: A Brief History of the Twenty-first Century*, Farrar, Straus and Giroux, 2005.

might take a whole decade to play out, now it's being played out within months. The world has fundamentally changed in terms of the cycle time, and the frequencies of these booms and busts. It's not going to be 50 years; it's been compressed. We have to plan to face these types of tsunamis on a periodic basis.'

What is your future? While you're putting out the fire think about where future fires will be. Says Henry Fernandez: 'In an environment like this, you're the captain of the fire team and you have your own hose putting out the fire. You're sitting there and you're trying to anticipate is the fire going to go to the next house, is it going to take the whole neighbourhood? So, leadership is about trying to figure out what is going to happen and how do you position yourself, even if you're in the middle of this horrendous crisis?'

And this brings us back to a leader's passion.

Setting an example

What does your face say? Bad news is a virus leaders cannot afford to spread. Henry Fernandez: 'To the leaders of the company, I always keep telling them it's not about you, it's about them. It's about the employees in front of you. If you have a bad day, you hide it, my friend, because you can be transmitting a virus. We are a very hard-charging company but we try to create an environment in which people take time off. We preach very aggressively that they should not focus on the papers, not focus on the financial markets, that they should relax when they can. When they're here there's a high level of intensity but they focus on the positives, focus on the benefit that we're going to get out of this crisis and I keep telling them, look, we know all the problems, we know that clients are going to go out of business, that products are going to get cancelled. All of that is a given. We know what it is. Let's focus on what we can improve.'

How do you look? How does what you are doing look to employees? Leadership is about setting an example 24/7. 'We know that because growth has slowed, bonus payments and the like will be lower, because the company has not met its goals. But the leadership example starts at the top. We cut the bonus for the top first, before anybody else gets affected', says Kris of Infosys.

Keeping the faith

How philosophical are you? Cycles happen. A solid business does not become a bad one overnight. There has to be a sense of realism to a leader's view of the turbulent world. 'So long as there are cycles they are going to affect you and you need to take them in your stride. Things will change and there is no need to reset your basic theses in terms of the growth opportunities', suggests K.V. Kamath.

As a final word, let's hear from Jeff Immelt, CEO of General Electric. We saw Immelt speak about his leadership challenges. His words struck an impressive chord. Watching Immelt talk, there is a sense of confidence and competence, rather than the heady scent of ego transmitted by many CEOs on the world stage. 'Running GE is a full-time job. I have had five days off in nine months', he admits. 'You need to be comfortable with yourself and being criticised. My advice to people is to do what you like. The thing I love about GE is that we're going to have a front seat in history whether it's in China or elsewhere.' Immelt is sitting comfortably but not complacently. He describes himself as optimistic but anxious about the future. 'We have a platform for real change and I am convinced GE will emerge as a better company.'

Much the same sentiments were expressed by many leaders we spoke to. They feel they have a front seat in history. They realise there is a choice: to *make* history or to become it.

Index

Acknowledgements

We would like to thank all those leaders who found time to talk to us about their own approach during these turbulent times. In particular, thanks are due to the following:

Talal Al Zain, CEO, Bahrain Mumtalakat Holding Company
Richard Baker, Chairman, Virgin Active
John Brock, Chairman and CEO, Coca-Cola Enterprises Inc.
Sam DiPiazza, Senior Partner, former Global Chief Executive Officer, PricewaterhouseCoopers
Edward Dolman, CEO, Christie's International
Carlos Fernandez, Chairman and CEO, Grupo Modelo
Henry Fernandez, Chairman and CEO, MSCI Barra
Tim Flynn, Chairman, KPMG International
Mark P. Frissora, CEO, Hertz Corporation
Victor Fung, Group Chairman, Li & Fung Group
Carlos Ghosn, President and CEO, Nissan; President and CEO, Renault
Tom Glocer, CEO, Thomson Reuters Corporation
Rick Goings, Chairman and CEO, Tupperware Brands Corporation
Kris Gopalakrishnan, CEO, Infosys Technologies Ltd
George Halvorson, Chairman and CEO, Kaiser Permanente
Wang Jianzhou, Chairman and CEO, China Mobile Limited
Kazuyasu Kato, CEO, Kirin Holdings

K.V. Kamath, Chairman, ICICI Bank
Bijan Khosrowshahi, former CEO, Fuji Fire & Marine
Seung-Yu Kim, CEO, Hana Financial Group
Yorihiko Kojima, President and CEO, Mitsubishi Corporation
Bruno Lafont, Chairman and CEO, Lafarge
Richard Langan, Managing Partner and CEO, Nixon Peabody
Anand Mahindra, Vice Chairman and Managing Director, Mahindra & Mahindra Ltd.
Chip McClure, Chairman, CEO, and President, ArvinMeritor
Alexey Mordashov, CEO, Severstal
James Owens, Chairman and CEO, Caterpillar
Takeshi Niinami, President and CEO, Lawson Inc.
Monika Ribar, President and CEO, Panalpina
Stuart Rose, CEO and Chairman, Marks & Spencer
Peter Sharpe, President and CEO, Cadillac Fairview Corporation
Jim Skinner, Vice-Chairman and CEO, McDonald's
Nick Stephan, founding Managing Director and CEO, Phoenix Partners Group
H. Patrick Swygert, former president of Howard University
Linda Wolf, former Chairman and CEO, Leo Burnett

Our thanks to Heidrick & Struggles board members Jill Kanin-Lovers and Gary Knell for their contributions and to Gerry Roche, Senior Chairman of Heidrick & Struggles.

Thanks to Alice Au, Arun Das Mahapatra, Daniel Edwards, Scott Eversman, Ayman Haddad, Elisabeth Marx, Stephen Miles, Luis Moniz, Toshifumi Mori, Juan

Ignacio Perez, Manoel Rebello and John Wood for their introductions to some of the CEO and Chairmen we spoke to.

Thanks also to our publisher Liz Gooster whose good advice and patience made this project fly.

The support and hard work of Tammy Frasz and Claire Davies is reflected in the number of interviews conducted and the insights we gained.

Finally, thank you to Stuart Crainer, without whom this book would not have been written.

About Berrett-Koehler Publishers

Berrett-Koehler is an independent publisher dedicated to an ambitious mission: Creating a World That Works for All.

We believe that to truly create a better world, action is needed at all levels—individual, organizational, and societal. At the individual level, our publications help people align their lives with their values and with their aspirations for a better world. At the organizational level, our publications promote progressive leadership and management practices, socially responsible approaches to business, and humane and effective organizations. At the societal level, our publications advance social and economic justice, shared prosperity, sustainability, and new solutions to national and global issues.

A major theme of our publications is "Opening Up New Space." They challenge conventional thinking, introduce new ideas, and foster positive change. Their common quest is changing the underlying beliefs, mindsets, institutions, and structures that keep generating the same cycles of problems, no matter who our leaders are or what improvement programs we adopt.

We strive to practice what we preach—to operate our publishing company in line with the ideas in our books. At the core of our approach is *stewardship*, which we define as a deep sense of responsibility to administer the company for the benefit of all of our "stakeholder" groups: authors, customers, employees, investors, service providers, and the communities and environment around us.

We are grateful to the thousands of readers, authors, and other friends of the company who consider themselves to be part of the "BK Community." We hope that you, too, will join us in our mission.

Be Connected

Visit Our Website

Go to www.bkconnection.com to read exclusive previews and excerpts of new books, find detailed information on all Berrett-Koehler titles and authors, browse subject-area libraries of books, and get special discounts.

Subscribe to Our Free E-Newsletter

Be the first to hear about new publications, special discount offers, exclusive articles, news about bestsellers, and more! Get on the list for our free e-newsletter by going to www.bkconnection.com.

Get Quantity Discounts

Berrett-Koehler books are available at quantity discounts for orders of ten or more copies. Please call us toll-free at (800) 929-2929 or email us at bkp.orders@aidcvt.com.

Host a Reading Group

For tips on how to form and carry on a book reading group in your workplace or community, see our website at www.bkconnection.com.

Join the BK Community

Thousands of readers of our books have become part of the "BK Community" by participating in events featuring our authors, reviewing draft manuscripts of forthcoming books, spreading the word about their favorite books, and supporting our publishing program in other ways. If you would like to join the BK Community, please contact us at bkcommunity@bkpub.com.